AF021
MASSIMILIANO AFIERO

AXIS FORCES
21

The Axis Forces 021 - First edition October 2022by Luca Cristini Editor for the brand Soldiershop
Cover & Art Design by soldiershop factory.   ISBN code: 978-88-93278928

The Axis Forces number 21 – September 2022

<u>Direction and editing:</u> Via San Giorgio, 11 – 80021 AFRAGOLA (NA) -ITALY

Managing and Chief Editor: Massimiliano Afiero

Email: maxafiero@libero.it - **Website**: www.maxafiero.it

Contributors

Tomasz Borowski, Grégory Bouysse, Stefano Canavassi, Carlos Caballero Jurado, Rene Chavez, Paolo Crippa, Carlo Cucut, Antonio Guerra, Lars Larsen, Christophe Leguérandais, Eduardo M. Gil Martínez, Michael D. Miller, Peter Mooney, Péter Mujzer, Ken Niewiarowicz, Erik Norling, Raphael Riccio, Hugh Page Taylor, Charles Trang, Cesare Veronesi, Sergio Volpe

Editorial

Sorry I'm late. Once again we have not been able to respect the timing of publication of our magazine and we are here to apologize to all our readers. Various logistical problems and above all the loss of numerous collaborators who for various reasons, especially health, were unable to contribute with their research work, did not allow us to complete the new issues of the magazine in time. We count in the future to be able to respect the timing of publication, managing to produce an issue every three months (four in a calendar year). We therefore ask everyone for greater collaboration, especially in pointing out and bringing to our attention topics of greatest interest to be discussed, again in the context of the Second World War and above all on the use of Axis units on the various war fronts. Meanwhile, the war in Ukraine is continuing and creating economic problems especially for European countries. We hope that everything ends as soon as possible. Let's now analyze the contents of this new issue of the magazine. We begin with the deployment of the Wiking Division in the Caucasus regions in the summer of 1942. Following is the biography of Bruno Hinz, an SS officer, who served first in the Wiking Division and then in the Götz von Berlichingen. We continue with the employment of the Italian volunteers who served in the Waffen-SS on the Nettuno front in the spring of 1944. We then return to talk about the Polizei Division, dealing with its operational employment on the Leningrad front between the summer of 1942 and January 1943. We conclude with an article dedicated to the Legionary War Cross, intended for French volunteers who fought on the Eastern Front alongside the German armed forces. Always hoping to have met your interest in military history, I wish everyone happy reading and see you in the next issue.

Massimiliano Afiero

Contents

in World War Two 1939-1945

The SS-Division Wiking on the Eastern Front Summer 1942

By Massimiliano Afiero

May 23, 1942, *SS-Gruppenführer* **Felix Steiner at his 46th birthday celebration.**

After having maintained their positions during the terrible winter of 1941-42, partly stemming the Soviet offensive along the entire Eastern Front, with the arrival of spring 1942 the German military strategists began to plan their next moves, focusing primarily on the southern front. New attacks against Moscow and Leningrad were temporarily put on hold; with the entry of the United States into the war, the Third Reich was in urgent need of raw materials, especially oil. The Soviets had large oil fields along the coast of the Caspian Sea and their capture became of vital importance. The objectives of the new offensive, codenamed *"Fall Blau"* (Plan Blue), set forth by Hitler in Directive Number 41 dated April 5, 1942, called for the annihilation of Soviet forces located between the Donetz basin and the Don, the capture of the Caucasus passes and the rich oil fields on the Caspian Sea. In addition, the new offensive also masked another objective which was much more ambitious: linking up with the Italo-German forces coming from Egypt and with Japanese forces coming from India. Doing so would have dealt a death blow to British economic and territorial interests in the Middle East and Asia Minor. The offensive, which was supposed to employ exclusively the forces of *Heeresgruppe Süd* (Army Group South), had been divided into four distinct operational phases: initially, the enemy defensive line along the Don was to be broken through at Voronezh (*Blau 1*), then capture the entire Don basin as far as the Donetz (*Blau 2*). Soon after, the German forces would be involved in the capture of the entire area between the Don, Stalingrad and Rostov (*Blau 3*). At that point, the attack was to shift to the south, with the aim of conquering the entire Caucasus region between the Caspian Sea, the Black Sea, the Volga River and the Caucasus mountain chain with its rich oil fields (*Blau 4*).

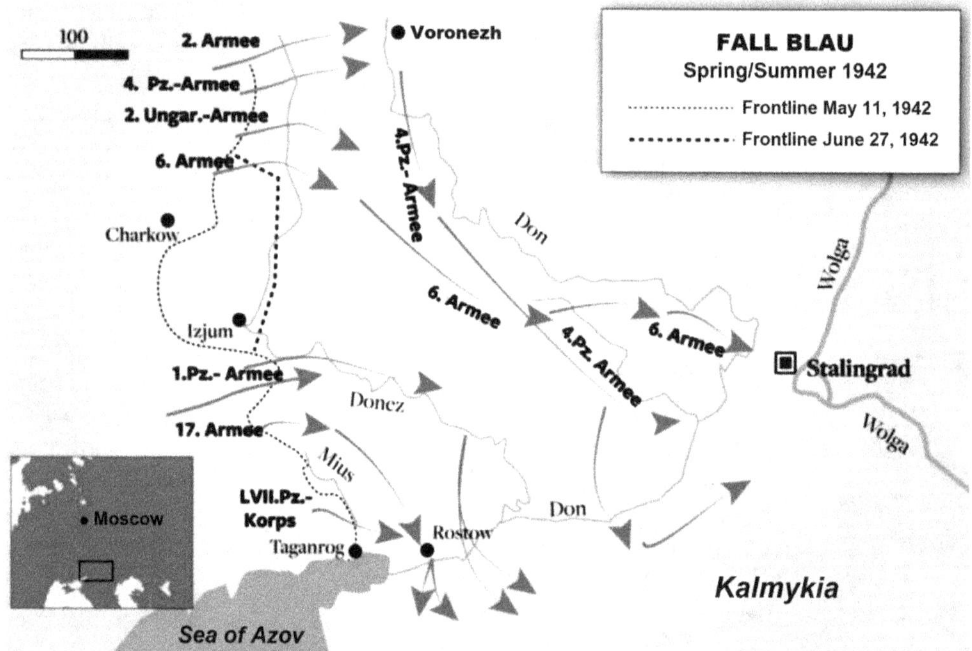

Movement of the front line between May and June 1942.

General Erich von Manstein.

Before launching the new offensive, however, it would be necessary to eliminate several dangerous Soviet salients that were wedged in the German defensive front, especially at Kharkov, Izjum and in the Kerch peninsula. In early May 1942, Soviet forces had launched their own offensive in the Izjum area, but were surrounded and completely wiped out, losing more than a thousand tanks, 2,500 guns and leaving more than 240,000 prisoners in German hands (Operation *Fridericus*). On the Crimean front, *11.Armee* under General von Manstein was able to conquer the entire peninsula. Between 10 and 26 June 1942, other offensive actions were carried out that enabled the German forces to establish a bridgehead on the eastern bank of the Donetz River to the east of Kharkov.

 in World War Two 1939-1945

Fall Blau

Operation Blue began officially on June 28, 1942, with German units advancing rapidly as they had the previous summer. The Soviets were overrun and forced to retreat everywhere. The first forces to move were those that were deployed in the Voronezh sector - in early July German armoured spearheads had crossed the Don River. The Soviets, however, were able to fall back in time to avoid being wiped out, digging in along a new defensive line further to the east. This unexpected retreat forced the German commands to review their plans, having to carry out the offensive along two different axes, with the resultant splitting of the forces committed. On July 9, in fact, the Army Group South was subdivided into new Army Groups, Army Group A, under Marshal Wilhelm List, and Army Group B, under Marshal von Weichs. Army Group A consisted of *17.Armee* under Ruoff, *4.Panzer-Armee* under Hoth and *1.Panzer-Armee* of von Kleist.

A German *PzKpfw.III* on the Eastern Front, Summer 1943.

Panzers **and half-tracks of 23.*Pz.Div.* on the move.**

The SS-Wiking Division was attached to *1.Panzer-Armee*. Army Group B consisted of von Salmuth's *2.Armee*, the *6.Armee* under Paulus, the Romanian Third and Fourth Armies, the Italian Eighth Army and the Hungarian Second Army. Hitler's new Directive Number 43, dated July 23, 1942, fixed the objectives of the German offensive along two clearly defined axes: Army Group B was to capture Stalingrad with a quick action (Operation *Fishereiher*, or Heron) and secure the left flank of Army Group A, which was to push into the Caucasus (Operation *Edelweiss*, Alpine Star).

Johannes Mühlenkamp in a 1941 photo.

A *PzKpfw.IV* of the *Wiking* (*Giorgio Bussano*).

The panzers of the Wiking

After having spent the winter along the course of the Mius, during the spring of 1942 the *Wiking* Division had been completely reorganized, thanks to the arrival of new reinforcements, especially a battalion consisting of Finnish volunteers and an armoured battalion, commanded by *SS-Stubaf.* Johannes Mühlenkamp. Its *1.* and *2.Kompanie* were equipped with *PzKpfw.III* tanks mounting the long-barrelled 50mm gun. Each company consisted of four platoons with four tanks plus a command tank, in which the unit commander fought. The two company commanders were *SS-Ostuf.* Schnabel of the First and *SS-Ostuf.* von Staden of the Second. The third company was equipped with *PzKpfw.IV* tanks armed with the short-barrelled 75mm gun. The unit was commanded by *SS-Hstuf.* Fritz. Darges. The *Stabskompanie*, under *SS-Ostuf.* Walter Geipel, consisted of the *Aufklärungszug* (reconnaissance platoon) led by *SS-Ustuf.* Josef "Sepp" Martin, equipped with *PzKpfw.II* light tanks, the *Kradschützenzug* (motorcycle platoon) under *SS-Ustuf.* Willi Hein, the *Pionierzug* under *SS-Ustuf.* Fritz Schraps and the *Nachtrichtenzug* (signals platoon) under *SS-Ustuf.* Hans Köntopp. The crews had trained intensively for many weeks. The armoured units reached the *Wiking* division at the end of June at Amrowsijewska, on the Mius front. On June 29, the commander of the Second Company, *SS-Ustuf.* Theodor von Staden, was mortally wounded during an exercise. Company command then passed to *SS-Ostuf.* Hans Flügel.

in World War Two 1939-1945

The *PzKpfw.II* tanks of the light reconnaissance platoon of *SS-Hstuf*. Martin, Summer 1942.

A *PzKpfw.III Ausf.L* of the *Wiking* (*Charles Trang*).

Orders for the Wiking

At the beginning of July, marching orders arrived for the *Wiking* Division. Its commander, Steiner, thus began to analyse them along with his chief of staff, *SS-Hstuf*. Erwin Reichel. On July 18, the division was to reach the area north-east of Taganrog, on the Sea of Azov, and establish a bridgehead on the other side of the Mius. From there it was to head towards Rostov and capture that city. Once Rostov had fallen, German forces would have free access to all of the western Caucasus. The march of the *Wiking* units to the south began on July 16, 1942, north-west of Taganrog. Despite the best efforts of the division's logistic services, only the units of the *"Germania"* and two battalions of *"Nordland"* were able

SS-Obf. **Fritz von Scholz.**

SS-Obf. **Jürgen Wagner.**

to be "motorized". The *"Westland"* and *III./Nordland* were not able to join the division until the end of July in the Maikop area. With the available motorized units, Steiner organized three combat groups, under Fritz von Scholz, commander of *Nordland*, Jürgen Wagner, commander of *Germania* and Otto Gille, commander of the *Wiking* artillery regiment. The *Kampfgruppe* commanded by *SS-Obf.* Gille was to lead the attack, and for that purpose was reinforced by Mühlenkamp's armoured battalion, in effect becoming a *Panzergruppe*. On July 19, units of *17.Armee* were able to break through Soviet positions west of Rostov, pushing *LVII.Panzer-Korps* ahead on the left and *V.Armee-Korps* on the right towards the Don, between the positions at Rostov and Batajsk. The *LVII.Panzer-Korps* under General Kirchner, consisting of the *Wiking* Division, the *13.Panzer-Division* and a Slovak division, headed directly towards Rostov in an attempt to take it by a surprise attack. At the same time, Rostov was attacked from the north by *III.Panzer-Korps* under General von Mackensen, consisting of *14.Panzer-Division* and *22.Panzer-Division*. During the night of 21 July 1942, the *Wiking* armoured battalion began to move. The motors sprang to life and the tanks began their march one after another, in the light of the summer dusk. Throughout the night, more than fifty tanks advanced towards the bridgehead at Ssambek that had been established by an army infantry division. After having covered some fifty kilometers, the tanks reached the village of Sultan-Saly. There, *SS-Stubaf.* Mühlenkamp was ordered to attack to the southwest of that location and then to continue to march on towards Rostov. The Wiking's panzers thus began their move towards the Don. Given the great strategic importance of Rostov, a key position at the mouth of the Don River, the Soviets had set up a formidable defensive ring around the city, characterized by a triple fortified line, comprising many anti-tank ditches that were three meters deep and six meters wide, thanks to labour provided by the civilian population of Rostov itself. The Germans had been forced to abandon Rostov the previous year and now, returning to attack it, they fully expected stiff resistance.

SS-Stubaf. **Mühlenkamp, Summer 1942.**

A *PzKpfw.III* of the *Wiking* on the march, 1942.

The march towards Rostov

SS-Ostuf. Ewald Klapdor, one of the platoon leaders in the 1st Company of the *Wiking* armoured battalion, was part of the first assault wave. On July 21, after the infantry units had managed to break through the Soviet defensive front north of Taganrog, the armoured units were ordered to exploit that success. The panzers of the *Wiking* went on the march during the night between 21 and 22 July to reach their attack positions, overcoming ditches and anti-tank obstacles, thanks to the great job done by the German engineers. All of the tank commanders, with their torsos exposed outside the turret hatches, attempted to check on the positions of their comrades in the glimmer of that summer night. There were anti-tank obstacles everywhere. It seemed that the entire sector had been organized to fend off an attack by tanks. Once the south-western part of Sultan-Saly was reached, the panzers took up positions behind a hill to protect themselves from Soviet artillery fire. The order to get ready to attack arrived shortly thereafter; the tank commanders climbed into their turrets again, closed the hatches and ordered the engines to be started. After having assumed the classic "W" combat formation, they moved towards the crest of the hill, where they had hidden themselves from the sight of the enemy. The uneven ground made the tanks and the crews inside them bounce. In the meantime, the first light of dawn had lightened up the battlefield. *SS-Ostuf.* Klapdor communicated via radio with his company commander, *SS-Ostuf.* Günter Schnabel, to report that everything was going well: *"..good visibility, no obstacles in sight"*. Nevertheless, after having covered a few more meters, Klapdor was forced to stop suddenly; the road was blocked by a minefield. All of a sudden there was an explosion and the tank seemed to lift off the ground. Klapdor's panzer had hit a mine and his radio operator was seriously wounded; there was no longer any radio and no-one to man the on-board machine gun in the event of an enemy attack.

Wiking **Panzers on the move on the Ukrainian steppe, Summer 1942.**

Wiking **Panzers on the move on the Ukrainian steppe, 1942.**

A *Wiking* **armoured formation on the attack, 1942.**

Klapdor immediately realized that the situation was serious. Through the periscope, the *SS-Obersturmführer* then began to scan the surrounding terrain to identify the locations of the Soviet anti-tank guns, which in the meantime had begun to take the German tanks under fire. Some panzers were able to respond to the fire and managed to knock out a few enemy guns. The driver did not lose his calm; he could not do much to help the radio operator who lay wounded alongside him, so he focused all of his attention on driving the tank. He had to avoid bouncing in order to enable the gunner to aim at and destroy the Soviet anti-tank guns. The tanks slowly emerged from the minefield without detonating any more mines. *SS-Ostuf.* Klapdor glanced to his left and to his right, everything seemed to be going well. The other three panzers in his platoon had cleared the minefield without any damage and the attack was able to continue. Suddenly his tank lurched forward violently. The members of the crew were slammed against the tank's interior.

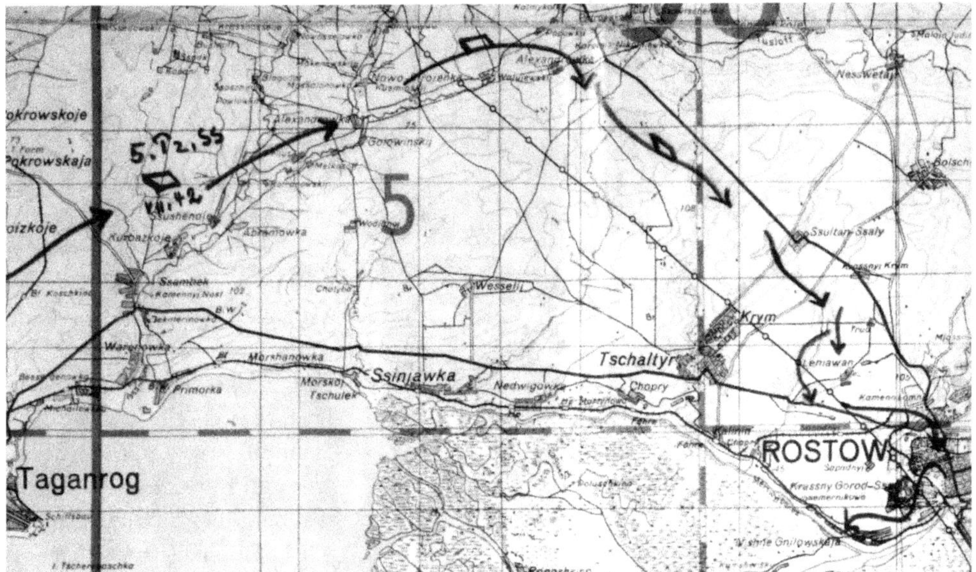

Route of march of the Wiking's *Panzer Abteilung* towards Rostov, Summer 1942.

A *PzKpfw.IV* of 3.*Kompanie* on the march, Summer 1942.

Then the vehicle came to a complete halt. Despite the efforts of the driver, the tank would no longer move, the engine roared but nothing was able to free the mass of steel from its trap. Once it was immobilized, Klapdor's tank was subjected to fire from Soviet heavy weapons; machine gun rounds rattled like hail on the tank's hull, making the inside of the tank shake. The turret had stuck when the *panzer* had fallen into a ditch. The radio operator was wounded and could not man the machine gun. Nothing could be seen from the periscope, except the ground in front and the sky to the rear. Klapdor could hear the sounds of the battle, a sign that the other tanks had continued on towards Rostov. He then decided to get out of the tank to see what was happening; he opened the turret hatch and jumped out, punctuating the occasion with a

A *SS-Wiking* armoured column on the march, Summer 1942.

In the turret, *SS-Oscha*. Eilers of *2.Panzer-Kompanie*.

loud chorus of curses. It was only then that he became aware that his tank had fallen into a well-camouflaged anti-tank ditch and the fall had been so brutal that the main gun had dug itself into the ground. How to get out of there? While the other crew members were giving first aid to the radio operator, Klapdor managed to stop one of the *Wiking* tanks of the second attack wave in order to pull his tank out of the ditch using a steel tow cable. When his tank was finally in the horizontal position once again, the crew put the turret and gun to rights and quickly resumed their march. Klapdor was impatient to catch up with the first assault wave and to resume his place at the head of his platoon. Going as fast as possible, his *panzer* was able to gain lost ground, heading towards the great anti-tank ditch that had to be crossed at all costs.

Combat engineers in action

Having reached the edge of the anti-tank ditch, the panzers of Mühlenkamp's battalion began to fire upon the Soviet positions on the other side of the ditch. Soon after, the combat engineers showed up in their Volkswagens loaded with explosives and all of the material need to cross the three enemy defensive belts. The engineers were ordered to catch up with the leading panzers and to clear a path for them.

Their vehicles threaded their way among the tanks, moving continuously to avoid being hit by enemy heavy weapons. After having made it through a minefield, they descended to the bottom of the gigantic anti-tank ditch. The panzers provided covering fire.

A *PzKpfw.III* of the Third Platoon of *1.Kp./SS-Pz.Abt.* *'Wiking'* immobile after having ended up in a ditch (*Charles Trang Collection*).

A *PzKpfw.III* of the *Wiking* during an attack, July 1942.

The engineers quickly placed their explosive charges to collapse the sides of the walls of the trench and to open a path for Mühlenkamp's tanks. A company of grenadiers arrived to complete the push to the other side. The SS troops of Dieckmann's assault battalion from the *"Germania"* jumped into the ditch and scaled it, reaching its eastern bank, establishing an initial bridgehead. The engineers had managed to establish a sort of ramp in the ditch, which however did not hold up for long, because the ground that was shaken by explosions gave way shortly thereafter. The *Waffen SS* engineers then requested assistance from *Luftwaffe* engineers, whose ramps were undoubtedly stronger, as they were used to build landing strips under all types of terrain conditions. The *Luftwaffe* engineers arrived soon afterwards and began to manhandle tree trunks and beams. The German volunteers came to admire their works as interested spectators; a layer of wooden beams, a layer of dirt, a new layer of beams and another layer of dirt. The bottom of the ditch was thus filled up a bit at a time. One of Mühlenkamp's panzers quickly tried to cross; as soon as it went down the slope, it slid forward causing half of the foundation, which could not support its weight, to give way.

SS-Wiking **panzers overrunning an enemy defensive position (*Charles Trang Collection*).**

A *PzKpfw.III* of 2.*Kompanie* and *Wiking* infantry.

The tank was barely able to turn around and return to the other side, all the while raising a huge cloud of dust. The *Luftwaffe* engineers then went back to work, assisted by their *Waffen SS* comrades, rebuilding the passageway, this time much more solidly. The minefields on both sides of the ditch had been cleared and the panzers finally were able to cross the obstacle, one after another, all the while being helped by the German engineers who, with shovels in hand, continued to fill in holes as they appeared along the way. Having gained the eastern bank of the barrier, the units

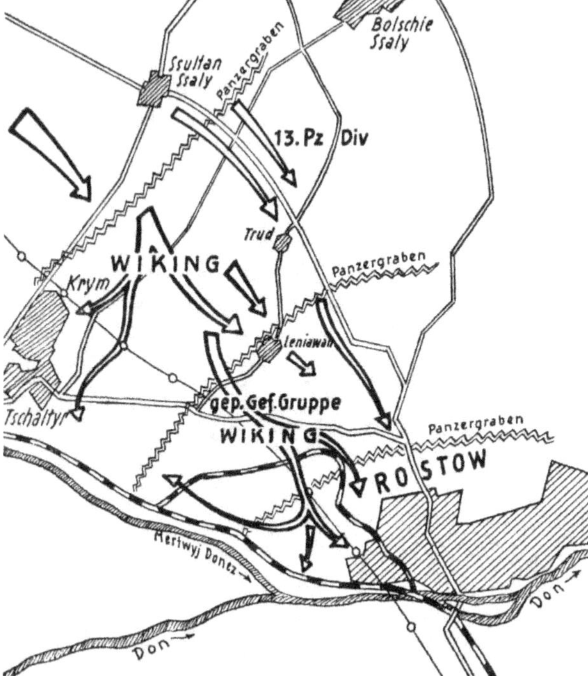

Map showing *SS-Wiking* approach routes to Rostov.

A *PzKpfw.III Ausf.J* of *1.Pz.Kompanie* clearing the ditch, assisted by engineers. *SS-Ostuf*. Klapdor is in the turret.

regrouped before beginning to chase the enemy forces, raising an immense cloud of smoke and dust. After having overrun the first Soviet defensive line, the German assault forces soon ran up against a second line. This time, however, the engineers, benefiting from their previous experience, were able to clear a path for the units in a short time. Stripped to the waist and bathed in sweat, the engineers went to work while the tankers waited impatiently, smoking cigarette after cigarette, wrapped in their black uniforms. Even the division staff were impatient; their orders were to proceed towards Rostov in all haste. A gigantic race had begun between the Germans and the Soviets. The Soviets were in dire straits after the fall of the first two anti-tank barriers.

Panzers attack

The German panzers continued to advance through the Ukrainian steppe, carrying out their march on Rostov. Occasionally, a Soviet artillery shell exploded among the tanks, but no-one paid any attention to them, as they were ineffective against the armour of their panzers. Always in the lead were the *PzKpfw.III* tanks of *1.Kompanie* commanded by *SS-Ostuf*. Schnabel. Following, covering the 1st, was *2.Kompanie* under *SS-Ostuf*. von Staden. *SS-Stubaf*. Hannes Mühlenkamp had thrown these two waves of about thirty tanks forward, which continued to protect each other as the situation warranted. Schnabel's tanks were engaged in wiping out the last pockets of resistance, machine guns and anti-tank guns, systematically destroying them one by one with their 50mm guns. Everything continued to go well; the panzers moved along at full speed, pausing only to fire, and then moved off again.

Engineers at work making it possible for tanks to cross, July 1942.

A PzKpfw.III Ausf.J of II.Zug of 1.Pz.Kompanie.

The enemy defensive positions were thus destroyed, one after another. *SS-Ostuf.* Schnabel's tank was in the rear, engaged in sweeping the area. The commander of *1.Kompanie* was not aware that an enemy anti-tank gun had him in its sights. Soon after, the Soviets opened fire, making a direct hit on the SS tank. The crew miraculously managed to get out of the burning vehicle in time. *SS-Ostuf.* Schnabel also escaped alive from the tremendous impact, suffering only some bruises and superficial wounds. His tank, however, was destroyed. Around nightfall, *SS-Stubaf.* Mühlenkamp spotted the houses and factories of Rostov on the horizon; huge clouds of smoke hung over the city. During the night, his panzers were resupplied with fuel and ammunition. The *Wiking* armoured battalion had been able to cross only two of the three defensive lines that protected Rostov.

The *PzKpfw.III* of *SS-Ustuf.* Max Kolodziey while it crosses the ditch (NARA).

SS-Stubaf. **Mühlenkamp and Dieckmann.**

Leninavan airport had been captured and the units had reached a new attack position north-west of Sapadny. From there, the attack against Rostov was to be kicked off the next day. *SS-Stubaf.* Mühlenkamp could only hope that the close cooperation would continue between his tankers and the combat engineers so that the final Soviet defensive line could be crossed quickly. They had made it through the minefields and anti-tank ditches twice already. Two thirds of the mission had been accomplished, but maybe the hardest part was yet to come. The closer the German forces got to Rostov, the stiffer the Soviet resistance became. At dawn on July 23, the panzers began their attack, the platoon led by *SS-Ustuf.* Wilde from *1.Kompanie* forging ahead with its four *PzKpfw.III*. Their 50mm guns soon began to hit the Soviet positions. The *SS-Untersturmführer* attacked an enemy artillery battalion consisting of six guns, wiping out gun after gun, thus clearing the way for his comrades who were then able to continue going forward without having to cope with fire from anti-tank guns. Wilde was able to break up the focal point of enemy resistance along the road to Rostov. The Wiking's panzers then found themselves facing the third and final Soviet anti-tank ditch.

SS-Ostuf. Pförtner, commander of 2.*Kp./Germania* and *SS-Stubaf.* Dieckmann, July 1942.

A group of dolsiers prior to resuming the attack. Motorcycle dispatch riders are bringing orders.

This time the Soviets had completed their work by adding railroad rails planted in concrete. They had to be demolished with explosives in order to continue the advance. The panzers and the grenadiers of Dieckmann's assault battalion advanced under protection of artillery and air cover. With this formidable array of power, the Germans were able to overcome all enemy resistance. The *"Stoffers"* and *"Polewacz"* battalions of the *"Nordland"* followed the mass of armour without encountering any resistance. The Soviets played their last cards in the defence of Rostov, but could do nothing stop the German panzers and infantry, who by now knew how to fight together in perfect synergy. The final obstacle was crossed in a rush.

Personnel of *Kampfgruppe Dieckmann*, tanks, half-tracks and motorcycles at a halt on the Ukrainian steppe while waiting for Stukas to hit the Soviet positions of the last defensive line, prior to moving on the attack, July 1942 (NARA).

SS-Panzermänner **standing on the turrets of their thanks for a better view of the horizon.**

In the early afternoon, the armoured battalion was ready to enter the city on the Don; Soviet resistance appeared to be completely broken. Fire and smoke were everywhere. The city, which was still far off, seemed deserted, as though petrified in smoke and ash. Very carefully, with their hatches buttoned up, Mühlenkamp's panzers entered the outskirts of the city, fighting alongside units of a *Wehrmacht* armoured division coming from another sector. Noise of fighting could be heard coming from the southern bank of the Don, where it divided into several branches, between which there were marshy fields.

A *PzKpfw.III* of 2.Kp./SS-Pz.Abt. *'Wiking'* passing through a Soviet defensive position.

A *PzKpfw.III* with infantry aboard, July 1942.

The tankers soon realized that the roads were blocked by barricades, so they ran the risk of becoming enmeshed in close-in fighting, which was always dangerous and deadly for armoured formations. *"Let's try to reach the bank of the Don south of the city"* Mühlenkamp said to his men. While the panzers distanced themselves from urban combat, the grenadiers of the *"Germania"* were busy taking the city house by house; guns and machine guns were emplaced at crossroads. At the same time that the last pockets of resistance in the city were being silenced, a German plane flew over the area dropping a message: German columns, withdrawing from the west, were trying to reach the western suburbs of Rostov. *"We'll try to cross the Don and get out of here!"* exclaimed Mühlenkamp. The commander of the Wiking's armoured battalion had not received any orders for some time and communication with the division headquarters had broken down. Nevertheless, he sent a message, even though he was not sure it would be received:"...*I am going to try to reach the banks of the Don and will*

 in World War Two 1939-1945

fight along the river". Rostov was in flames. The grenadiers of *1.Kompanie* led by *SS-Hstuf.* Hans Dorr of Dieckmann's battalion arrived in the city to find all of the bridges destroyed.

Another *PzKpfw.III* with infantry aboard, July 1942.

***Wiking* tanks on the outskirts of Rostov (*C. Trang*).**

Tanks and motorcycles from *Wiking* into Rostov.

Neither infantry nor tanks could cross to the southern bank of the river, so they began to establish total control along the entire northern bank while waiting for the engineers to build crossing points. The panzers attacked in the direction of the hamlet of Kalinine, enabling a *Wehrmacht* infantry division to complete the capture of the city. The Soviets continued to fight stubbornly, especially members of the NKVD, Stalin's dreaded secret police. These special units had been particularly trained for urban guerrilla warfare and gave their enemies a very rough time. Fighting in the centre of the city continued with even greater violence the next day, with the NKVD troops desperately defending the government buildings, having transformed them into veritable fortresses. When it came to defending their own headquarters, the fighting was so bitter that they fought to the last man rather than surrendering. Once the largest pockets of resistance had been eliminated, the *Wiking* grenadiers continued to be engaged in mopping up within the city to completely wipe out enemy units that still hung on.

Tank '311' of *SS-Ustuf.* Rolf Dedelow, supporting infantry of *I./Germania*, during a sweep on the northern bank of the Don, in the western suburbs of Rostov (*Charles Trang Collection*).

SS-Gruppenführer Felix Steiner on a defensive position, Summer 1942.

In the end, massive carpet bombing of neighbourhoods that continued to "hold out" by the *Luftwaffe* was necessary in order to eliminate the smouldering embers of resistance in the city. It was only then that Rostov fell totally under control of the German armed forces. The city represented not only an important port and a vital road and rail hub, but Rostov was also within reach of the Caucasus.

Towards the Caucasus

Once Rostov had fallen and the Don had been crossed, the German forces of Army Group A went on a wild fast race across the steppe in order to deny the Soviets the time to organize a defence of the Caucasus, digging themselves in along the Kuban River. To that end, attacks were made in depth to surround and destroy the Soviet forces that

in World War Two 1939-1945

had escaped across the Don south and south-east of Rostov. But the Soviets had become more experienced and decided to take advantage of their best ally, the vast expanse of the eastern steppes. The countryside was so vast that it was impossible to maintain control over the conquered territory. The German response was simple: move forward, as far and as quickly as possible, overrun enemy resistance, move through the villages, infiltrate between enemy lines like arrows.

SS-Stubaf. **Mühlenkamp's tank in the top photo, on the hills west of Rostov, followed by tank '122', in the bottom photo** (*Charles Trang Collection*).

For *SS-Gruf.* Felix Steiner, as with all of the other generals involved in that mad dash, everything looked simple. As Steiner himself explained to his chief of staff, Reichel: *"... we have to conquer half a thousand kilometers of steppe, and then we'll be in the Caucasus"*.

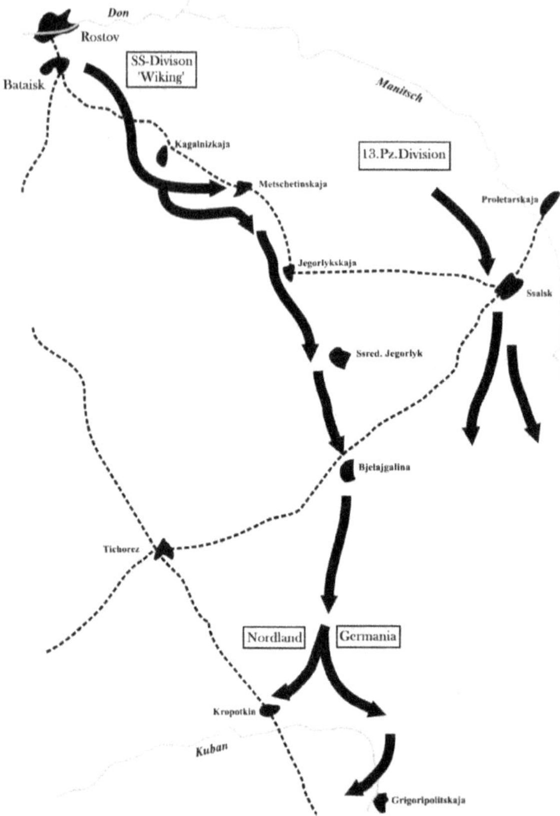

Wiking and *13.Panzer-Division* advance, Summer 1942.

Panzers from *Wiking* crossing an anti-tank ditch south of Rostov, with the assistance of engineers (*C. Trang*).

In reality it was an enormous objective, from the Black Sea to the Caspian Sea, one of the largest mountain chains in the world, the link between Europe and Asia. For their part, the Soviets were not well disposed to leaving the mountain route open to the enemy; every river and every stream was transformed into a defensive line upon which resistance could be anchored. With a few courageous soldiers, who certainly were not lacking in the Red Army, entire enemy companies could be stalled. The march of Army Group A to the south began with the conquest of the coastal area along the Black Sea; especially engaged in these operations were the motorized units of *1.Panzer-Armee* along the Armavir-Maikop axis, while the army under Ruoff, with *LVII.Panzer-Korps* commanded by General Kirchner, began to advance along the Novorossisk-Tuapse axis, with the aim of reaching Batumi. The *XXXIX.Geb.-Armee-Korps* under General Konrad was ordered to make a wide encircling move the Caucasus mountain passes with the aim or reaching Tuapse and Sukumi. Felix Steiner soon realized that his division of Germanic volunteers had entered into a new world. The *Wiking* Division left Europe for Asia, following along the course of the Manytsch River, which marked the border between the two continents. The first objective was to seize Bataisk, along the southern bank of the Don River, and to create a bridgehead from which a new offensive thrust could be launched. The weather was beautiful, the sun warmed everything. The columns dragged on from one well to another, like nomads in the desert. The SS soldiers hung their steel helmets from their belts, fashioning a new type of head gear similar to that of mountain troops, but using the same cloth used for their reversible camouflage combat jackets.

The *Kraderkundungszug* of the *Stabskompanie* of *SS-Aufkl.-Abt.* *'Wiking'* on the march (*Tiquet*).

Soldiers of the *Wiking*, Summer 1942.

German tanks, trucks and motorcycles crossed the wide river, finally reaching Bataisk. Dysentery began to claim many victims; after all was said and done, war was not only glory and blood, but mud and misery as well. On July 28, 1942, around nine at night, the forward elements of *Wiking*, still with Mühlenkamp and Dieckmann in the lead, ran into stiff enemy resistance near Kagalnizkaja, south-east of Rostov. A Soviet rear guard unit seemed determined to sacrifice itself on the spot in order to slow down the enemy advance and to give friendly units time to fall back to the Kuban. Throughout the night, German artillery shelled the enemy positions, and at dawn on July 29, the advance was able to resume. The *Waffen SS* soldiers saw the tanks of the *13.Panzer-Division*, who had been ordered to proceed to the east and capture Salsk, at the door to

Asia, pass in front of them. The Germanic volunteers were instead to continue marching to the south, in the direction of the Kuban.

Elements of *Gefechtsgruppe Gille* during a pause. In the foreground, with the flag, is *SS-Stubaf.* Mühlenkamp's command tank (*Charles Trang*).

Wiking advaced scouts scanning the horizon.

On the march towards Asia

The countryside changed quickly, it was no longer the Ukraine, but a strange world where the inhabitants had dark hair and laughed heartily. The villages were pleasant and full of flowers, the fields were red and yellow: tomatoes and corn. The attack by the German forces coincided with the harvest season for the fruit. Tanks and trucks moved through pear and apple trees. The fruits were enormous, full of juice and sun. The soldiers filled their bellies until they gorged themselves. For Steiner, however, this was not a pleasure trip; to reach the Kuban River as quickly as possible had become almost an obsession for him.

(To be continued)

Bibliography
Massimiliano Afiero, "*The SS-Division Wiking in the Caucasus 1942-1943*", MMPbooks
Massimiliano Afiero, "*5.SS-Panzer-Division Wiking volume I, 1941-1943*", Ass. Cult. Ritterkreuz

SS-Hauptsturmführer Bruno Hinz

By Peter Mooney

Bruno Hinz as an early war *Unterscharführer*.

Born in Petersdorf on the 25th if August 1915, he initially joined the SA in April 1933. He followed this by spending time in the R.A.D. This was from the start of April until the end of September 1936; he then joined the SS at the start of October. His first unit was Regiment *Deutschland*, serving with their 10th Company. He took part in the Austrian and Sudetenland pre-war campaigns and earned the medals for them. He fought in the west in 1940 and earnt the Second Class Iron Cross on the 18th of June 1940, this is also where he was wounded for the first time. He was promoted to *SS-Unterscharführer* in late-September 1940 and then spent time with the Replacement Battalion from December 1940 through to March 1941. He was awarded the Infantry Assault Badge at the start of April 1941,

the same day that he was posted to the officer's school at Braunschweig and stayed there until the end of September; he was assigned the SS number 313 698 whilst there. He was back at the front line before the end of that year, serving with *Wiking* and was awarded the First Class Iron Cross on the 2nd of December 1941. He was promoted to *SS-Untersturmführer* at the end of January 1942. The Russian Front Medal came on the 8th of September 1942. 1943 was a busy time for Hinz. The Silver Wound Badge was awarded to him at the start of April, followed quickly on the 15th of that month with the German Cross in Gold, which was for his company leadership within SS-Regiment *Westland*. Being wounded further, he spent time with SS-Replacement Battalion 5 in Klagenfurt from the 26th of May until late July 1943, when he went back to *Wiking* at the front line. The award of the Close Combat Clasp in Silver came on the 9th of August, then on the 27th of

A postcard signed by Hinz with the *Ritterkreuz*.

Wiking's soldiers on the Eastern Front, 1943.

September he received a serious lung wound that removed him from front line service again. This fourth wound resulted in multiple operations and a 6-month spell in hospital and recovery.

Knight's Cross

In late October, he was put forward for the award of the Knight's Cross by his Battalion Commander for actions conducted in early September. That document contained the following information: '*Positioned southwest of Kharkov, at the beginning of September 1943, the enemy threw heavy infantry and tank forces towards them, supported by artillery of all calibers, as well as howitzers. In this fighting they tried to break through our own lines towards Poltawa, in order to split us to the southeast and send our own forces back. The Regiment had to move their Platoons around during the course of this fighting, due to the strong enemy pressure that lasted for weeks. They continuously defended the positions north of the line Kharkov – Poltawa, between Bf. Schljach and Bortschany. Some of the hardest fighting during these days was before the 2./SS-Pz.Gren.Rgt Westland, under the command of SS-Untersturmführer Bruno Hinz, who lay before the location of Hf. Buzkij and the surrounding ground. Violent enemy fire from all calibres fell upon their own equipment, as well as salvo fire and aerial attacks. The enemy attacked several times on the 4.9.43 with strong infantry and tank support in an attempt to cut-off the* 2./SS-Pz.Gren.Rgt Westland. *They fought in hard close combat, under the personal actions of* SS-Untersturmführer *Hinz and his men, through which he spurred them on again and again by his*

Wiking's soldiers on the Eastern Front, 1943.

personal example to the highest achievements, rejecting the enemy with high bloody losses. By these repeatedly strong enemy attacks with all men and weapons, the connection to the neighbouring units of the Battalion was for a long time interrupted. A breakthrough by the enemy towards Walki was clearly recognised by Hinz, following which, he led the remainder of his Company again to a defense of these positions. From this calm resolution and the measures he repeadetly employed at the different points of enemy break-in, fighting at the head of his men, the enemy were thrown back. Leading the machine-gun troops, they removed enemy machine-guns themselves and he repeatedly struck hard at these enemy breeches, repelling the enemy. With renewed success the enemy attacked at the open flanks of the 2./SS-Pz.Gren.Rgt. Westland and broke into the rear of the Company. Protecting the mass of the Company against further frontal attacks, Hinz again threw himself against the enemy, leading his men. They destroyed this enemy again during bitter close combat. The personal bravery of SS-Untersturmfuhrer Hinz spurred his men again and again onto even higher achievements. During the multiple attacks by the enemy tanks, they let them roll past, they then completely smashed the enemy infantry who were following behind. By this determined initial defense and the unparalleled bravery of SS-Untersturmführer Hinz, also their resolute, determined and thorough counter-attacks, the enemy Platoons suffered heavy bloody losses. This allowed a reorganization of the Battalion, who reoccupied the main battle line and prevented the threat of the enemy break-in. SS-Untersturmfhrer Hinz took part in the campaign in the east and from the 28.12.42 was a Company Commander. He has always shown a high measure of bravery and fighting readiness, also distinguished himself through prudent leadership and exemplary attitude. He was distinguished in April of this year with the German Cross in Gold. I hold that SS-Untersturmführer Hinz is particularly worthy of the distinguishing of the award of the Knight's Cross of the Iron Cross.'

There is a separate document written by Gille on the 2nd of November, warmly approving this recommendation and emphasising the importance of his actions during the recent fighting. On the 9th of November he was promoted to *SS-Obersturmführer*, whilst recovering from his wounds. The award of the Knight's Cross came on the 2nd of December 1943. That award was approved whilst he was recovering from wounds received on the eastern front.

Oakleaves

He was listed as being with the SS-Training and Replacement Battalion 5 at that stage and he remained under them until the 10th of February 1944, when he moved to the *17. SS-Panzergrenadier Division 'Gotz von Berlichingen'*, commanding their 2nd Company with the *SS-Panzergrenadier Regiment 38*. It was with them that he conducted actions in the Normandy fighting, which resulted in his Divisional Commander (Otto Baum) writing a recommendation for the addition of the Oakleaves. That was compiled on the 21st July 1944 and read as follows: 'SS-Obersturmführer *Hinz was positioned with his Company at the swamp on the Taute-Kanal, projecting prominently from Graignes with his defensive front to the east, north and west. On the 10.7.44, Company Hinz was attacked by a strong enemy infantry and armour force, which continued south towards their reduced Battalion. SS-Obersturmführer Hinz gathered his Company and attacked on his own initiative, piercing behind this enemy. He brought heavy losses upon them, dispersing individual groups, which were attacking their Battalion. Hinz led an attack to the south, he then came across the strong enemy armoured force, which he did not want his Battalion to engage with. He then decided to go to the south, under cover, then go west across the wide marshy land with many moats and streams running through it. The completing of his decision was only possible the following night. Until then, Hinz defended himself with his Company in a hedgehog position, and with the onset of dusk, moved forward towards the enemy, westwards into the swamp. The difficulties of the land, especially overcoming the many stream sections, allowed the Battlegroup to advance only slowly, under heavy artillery fire. Hinz decided to halt and wait until the day was brighter, then determine through reconnaissance, where best to advance, at night to find a link with his Battalion. The*

SS-Ostuf. **Hinz with Oakleaves.**

Battlegroup was continually attacked in the swamp by enemy artillery and aircraft throughout the day. Because of the high grass and marsh, the traces of the night breakthrough were concealed. On the following night, Hinz led his complete Battlegroup back to their own Battalion. It is only thanks to the self-determined actions of SS-Obersturmführer *Hinz that the Battlegroup, with the strength of 100 men, found their way back to their own troops. Hinz, who suffers from an old injury that broke out again, due to standing for long hours in the water, has shown the highest measure of courage and determination. I think* SS-Obersturmführer *Hinz is worthy of the award of the Oakleaves to the Knight's Cross.'*

Adolf Hitler personally presenting Bruno Hinz with the Oakleavest to the Knight's Cross.

That proposal for the addition of the Oakleaves was approved on the 23rd August 1944, giving *Götz von Berlichingen* their first set of Oakleaves. It is worth noting that, just prior to that proposal being written, Hinz had been approved for the award of the Gold Wound Badge; on the 18th of July 1944. He had been wounded again, during this more recent figthting and was sent from the frontline, to recover in hospital. Whilst there, he was awarded the Close Combat Clasp in Gold, on the 5th of September. A promotion to *SS-Hauptsturmführer* followed on the 9th of November 1944. As part of his recovery and also due to him holding these prestigious awards, he went to Bad Tolz from the 21st November 1944 until the 20th January 1945. He had constantly requested a return to the front, despite the impact of his many wounds (nine listed during the war!) and he got his request on the 20th of January, when he was back with *Götz von Berlichingen*, in command of the *I. Bataillon, SS-Pz.Gren.Rgt. 38.* He remained with them as they fought in southern Germany, up to the surrender. He survived the war (some sources list him as having committed suicide at the end of the war), but the effects of his multiple injuries continued to plague him until his death on the 28th of February 1968.

Bibliography
"Waffen-SS Knights and their Battles – Volume 3 (August to December 1943)", Peter Mooney. Schiffer Publishing, 2012
"Waffen-SS Knights and their Battles – Volume 5 (June to August 1944)", Peter Mooney. Loyalty and Honour Publishing, 2020

The Nettunia Front, 1944

By Massimiliano Afiero

In January 1944, during the long advance up the Italian peninsula, the American forces of the 5th Army had reached the German Gustav defense line, which ran along the Garigliano River. Encountering stiff resistance, especially in the Cassino sector and along the Rapido River, the Allied headquarters planned to strike the rear of the German forces, landing an expeditionary corps on the shore between Anzio and Nettuno; at that time the two communities had been unified as a single municipality called Nettunia.

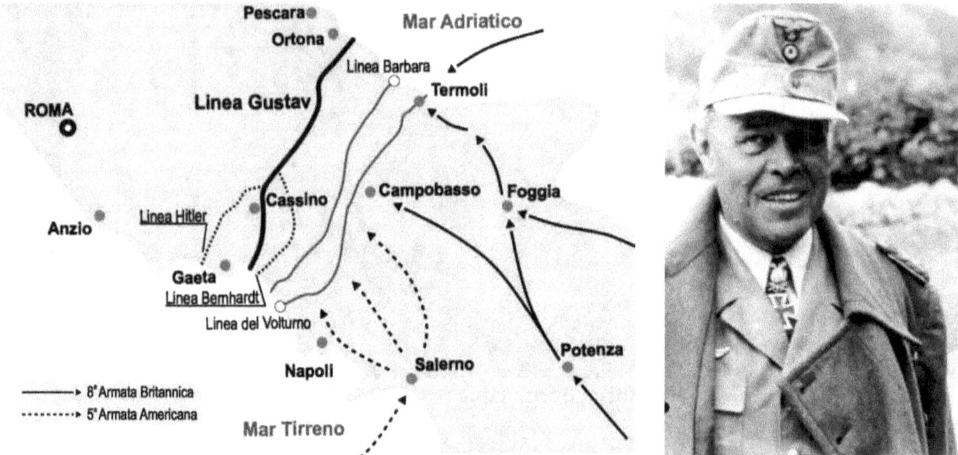

Left, advance of Allied forces toward Rome and German defensive lines. Right, *Feldmarschall* Albert Kesselring.

Allied troops on the Lazio coast, January 1944.

The VI Corps under General Lucas was to have landed behind the German lines at the same time as there was to be a frontal attack launched against the Cassino sector. In this way the VI Corps would have cut the German lines of communication between Rome and Cassino and isolated the German 10th Army. The first landings took place on January 22, 1944 (Operation *Shingle*) and by the next day fifty thousand Allied soldiers were on dry land: Allied VI Corps consisted of the British 1st Division, the US 45th Infantry Division, plus numerous US ranger and British commando units. The Germans had very few forces in the sector. Shortly following the Allied landings, it was possible only to send a few *Flak*

Troops and amphibious craft landing, January 1944.

SS-Gruf. Max Simon, commander of *16.SS-Pz.Gren.Div.* *'RF-SS'*, with other officers in Ljubljana, January 1944.

German *Panther* at the bridgehead, February 1944.

and artillery units and some armored vehicles to the area. But the Germans improvised quickly to send all of the available forces they could, taking advantage of the fact that Lucas, the American general, instead of quickly pushing inland, wanted to wait for the landing of heavy artillery and tanks. That same day of January 22 at the bridgehead, Feldmarschall Kesselring shifted troops of the *4.Fallschirmjäger-Division* stationed in Perugia and the *Fallschirm-Panzer-Division 'Hermann Göring'* stationed in the Priverno area in the province of Latina to the bridgehead. The *16.SS-Pz.Gren.Div.* *'Reichsführer SS'* was still being organized and with its men scattered between Italy and Slovenia, was also alerted. On the morning of that same day of January 22, the order reached the headquarters of the SS division to form two combat groups to transfer to subordination of the new *14.Armee* commanded by General von Mackensen (*I.Fallschirmkorps* and *LXXVI Panzer-Korps*), which faced the bridgehead. The first *Kampfgruppe* was formed with elements of *II./SS-Pz.Gr.Rgt.35* commanded by *SS-Sturmbannführer* August Dieterichs, consisting of veterans of the *Sturmbrigade* , while the second was formed with personnel of *II./SS-Pz.Gr.Rgt.36*, stationed at Ljubljana and initially commanded by *SS-Sturmbannführer* Fritz Knöchlein, and then from mid-March by *SS-Hstuf.* Herbert Vetter. The march of the two *Kampfgruppen* to the combat area was quite confused, especially that of *Kampfgruppe Knöchlein*, both because of the lack of enough transport as well as because

SS-Stubaf. August Dieterichs.

SS-Ostubaf. Fritz Knöchlein.

of the bad weather conditions and Allied aviation. The leading elements of *Kamfgruppe Dieterichs*, billeted at Lucca, arrived in the area as early as January 24. The two *Kampfgruppen* did not complete their moves until the end of January and were deployed along the Mussolini Canal (now the High Water Canal) between Borgo Podgora and Borgo Flora, subordinate to *715.Infanterie-Division. Reichsführer-SS* troops did not take part in the German counteroffensive that began on February 16 (Operation *Fischfang*) that attempted to annihilate the enemy forces that had landed, which developed in the area between Cisterna and Fosso della Moletta, in the northern part of the bridgehead. They were instead engaged in limited attacks against American forces (the 504th Paratroop Regiment) deployed along the Mussolini Canal, particularly the SS grenadiers of *Kampfgruppe Knöchlein*. Even though they were supported by several army assault guns, the SS companies suffered heavy losses, but nevertheless their action prevented the American paratroopers from sending reinforcements to the sector between Cisterna and Aprilia. On February 28, another attack was carried out by a company of *Kampfgruppe Dieterichs* towards the crossroads south of Borgo Flora, while another company of *Kampfgruppe Knöchlein* was to seize the bridge over the Mussolini Canal north of Borgo Podgora. Neither objective was taken mainly because of the small size of the forces engaged in the actions.

Arrival of Italian units

Shortly after the Allied landings between Anzio and Nettuno, the Duce, Benito Mussolini, expressly requested Kesselring immediately to send Italian SS units to the bridgehead. Kesselring replied a few days later, informing the Duce that *SS-Ogruf.* Wolff had already authorized the immediate outfitting and arming of the Italian SS troops and their movement to the front line, along with paratrooper personnel of the Nembo who had also joined the German side. In fact, as early as February 12 the first contingent of Italian paratroopers reached the bridgehead. On March 3, it was the turn of the *Barbarigo* naval infantry battalion of the X Divisione MAS to be deployed in the southern part of the front. Its First Company fought alongside men of Kampfgruppe Knöchlein. Aware that employment of the Italian SS units was being delayed, the Duce again requested their immediate dispatch to the combat zone. Thus, around mid-February *SS-Ogruf.* Wolff

     in World War Two 1939-1945

Milan, 'Adriatica' barracks, March 1944. From the left: *Ustuf*. Pio Filippani-Ronconi, *Ostubaf*. Carlo Federigo degli Oddi and *Leutnant der Schutzpolizei* Karl Häsecker, liaison officer in *1.Kompanie*.

A *Kampfgruppe Dieterichs* defensive position on the Anzio front, March 1944.

ordered the headquarters of the Italian SS legions to quickly form a new battalion of the *1.Sturmbrigade* to be employed on the southern front against the Allies. Therefore *SS-Standartenführer* Karl Diebitsch was charged with forming a *Kampfgruppe* consisting of the three battalions of *Infanterie-Regiment 1* of *1.Sturmbrigade*; the best personnel were concentrated in the II Battalion led by *Ostubaf*. Carlo Federigo degli Oddi, structured with three companies and a headquarters company. In the end, this was the only unit that was able to be prepared for the front, subordinate to *Kampfgruppe Diebitsch*, along with a support unit and a field hospital. The III Battalion served to provide replacements for the 'degli Oddi', while the *I.SS-Bataillon Debica* was engaged in anti-partisan operations until the end of May 1944. On the eve of its departure from Milan, the battalion consisted of 32 officers, 93 NCOs and 525 men. The volunteers were armed with 421 91/38 carbines, 131 Beretta MAB submachine guns, 130 Beretta pistols, 50 Breda model 30 light machine guns, 12 Breda model 37 heavy machine guns and 10 81mm mortars. There was also a German liaison element with the unit consisting of Schutpolizei officers and several interpreters. The unit left Milan by train on 13 March and did not arrive south of Rome until a week later, during the night of March 19-20. The area of the front was reached by truck where *Kampfgruppe Diebitsch* was assigned to *LXXXVI Panzer-Korps* and attached tactically to *715.Infanterie-Division*. The Italian SS troops took up positions between two combat groups of the '*Reichsführer-SS*'; the first to go into the line were the grenadiers of *1.Kompanie* under *Hstuf.* Buldrini, in the *II./SS-Pz.Gr.Rgt. 35* sector. The next day, *2.* and *3 Kompanie* were assigned to the *II./SS-Pz.Gr.Rgt. 36* sector.

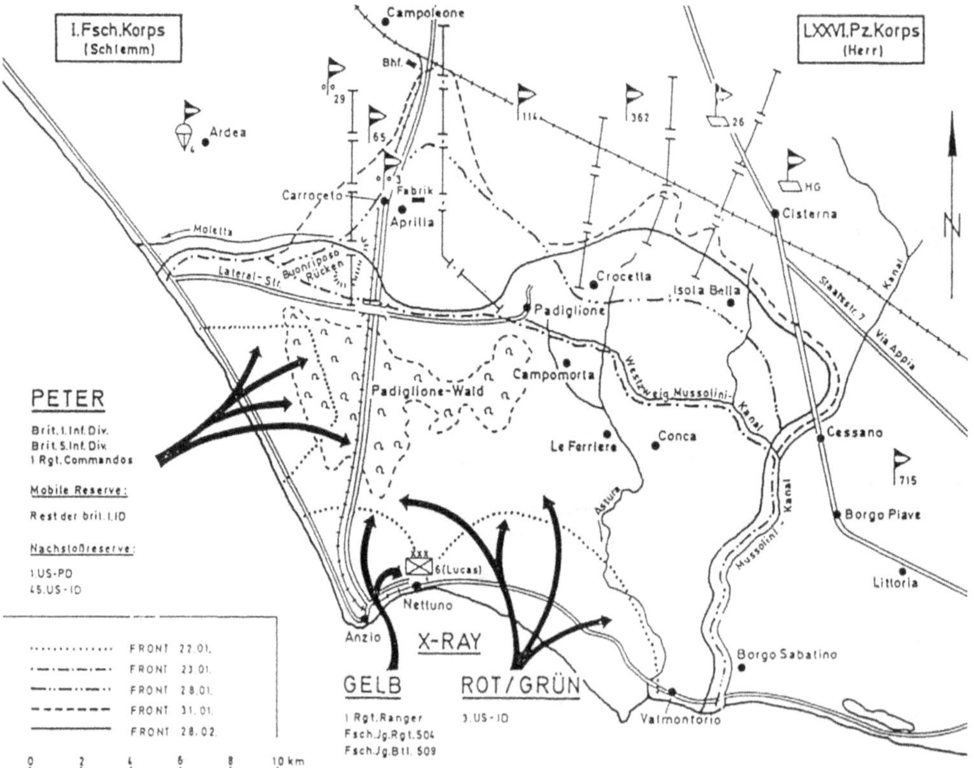

Map of the bridgehead with the front-line trace between January and February 1944.

German soldiers in the Anzio bridgehead.

Several platoons of *2.Kompanie* relieved the 1st company of the *Barbarigo*, in positions along the Mussolini Canal, veterans of terrible fighting in which they had taken heavy casualties. The choice of the sector assigned to the Italian SS troops was not by chance; the German headquarters selected a relatively quiet sector of the front to better integrate the Italian volunteers into the German defense scheme and to that end were positioned alongside SS troops of the '*Reichsführer*', who were considered most reliable.

German defensive positions on the Anzio front, March 1944: they appear to be like first World War trenches.

German soldiers under enemy fire, May 1944.

Of the Italian companies, only *3.Kompanie* led by *Hstuf.* Comini was given its own sector of the front, inserted between the positions of *5.* and *7.Kompanie* of *II./SS-Pz.Gr.Rgt. 36* (*Kampfgruppe Knöchlein*). The two other companies were split into platoons that were assigned to various companies of the '*Reichsführer-SS*', in particular, those of *1.Kompanie* among the companies of *Kampfgruppe Dieterichs* and those of *2.Kompanie* among those of *Kampgruppe Knöchlein*.

The headquarters of the Italian SS battalion and the support detachment assumed positions near Sermoneta, while the field hospital was set up at Abbadia. The defensive line along which the Italian volunteers were engaged ran along the Mussolini Canal and the Fosso di Cisterna; this line was protected by barbed wire and minefields, with many forward positions defensed by legionnaires. The first real obstacle to deal with was the nature of the terrain, which was damp and wet, which made it impossible to dig holes deep enough to provide cover from enemy fire. The Germans greeted the Italians quite reluctantly and it was only the test of fire that made them change their minds. The Italian legionnaires fought without ever being relieved, in an unnerving war of position in wet foxholes, engaged mainly in reconnaissance missions and raids behind enemy lines. In addition to those who fell in combat, rheumatic illness and malaria

Ustuf. **Filippani-Ronconi.** (*Filippani-Ronconi*)

Photos of Italian *Waffen SS* **volunteers taken by** *SS-Kriegsberichter* **Grönert on the Anzio front in 1944.**

also took their toll. To better coordinate actions against enemy positions, an Arditi Platoon was formed, consisting of some thirty men of the *1.Kompanie,* commanded by *Ustuf.* Filippani-Ronconi and *Ustuf.* Nicandro Bovenzi. During a night action at Borgo Flora on April 14, *Ustuf.* Filippani-Ronconi was seriously wounded by a mine. His place was taken by *Hscha.* Cavicchi, who was killed in combat at the end of May. Filippani-Ronconi was the first volunteer from the battalion to be awarded the Iron Cross Second Class. Six other Italian legionnaires received the same award shortly thereafter. On the pages of issue 4 of Avanguardia, the Italian SS newspaper, the first article on the employment of the Italian SS appeared: '*On the Nettuno front, during the course of patrol actions and enemy infiltration attempts, units of the Italian SS Legion decisively counterattacked and quickly re-established the prior situation. The volunteers of the new Italy, tested by fire, demonstrated excellent combat spirit and great morale*'.

On April 15, troops of the '*Reichsführer-SS*' were pulled from the front line. They were replaced by troops from *715.Infanterie-Division.* The Italian SS troops remained in their same positions. During the night of April 28-29, the Arditi Platoon was engaged in retaking a strongpoint near Borgo Flora. The Americans were thrown from the position, leaving seven prisoners in Italo-German hands. An enemy counterattack made about an hour later by an American company supported by armored vehicles and artillery fire was quickly repulsed. *Ustuf.* Bovenzi was wounded in the action. To face off against the enemy tanks, the Italian volunteers were instructed in the use of the *Panzerfaust* while the brigade headquarters received six 75mm Pak 40 antitank guns with their crews. To make up for the heavy losses sustained during the fighting (after a month about a hundred and fifty men were out of combat, among whom were thirty killed), *Ostubaf.* degli Oddi was 'forced' to accept about fifty volunteers who arrived directly at the front, almost all of whom were very young. Reinforcements later arrived from the brigade, mainly from III./R.1.

The Iron Cross...

(From issue 7 of Avanguardia, dated 29 April 1944)

In only a few weeks on the front line the volunteers of the Italian SS Legion have so distinguished themselves that five of them were awarded the Iron Cross Second Class in the field. Colonel Brigadier Diebitsch sent us correspondence regarding the ceremony for the award of the Iron Cross as well as his visit to our wounded. In the letter addressed to our editors he writes that the Italian volunteers are well and fight even better, even though in the last few days the battle has become bitter. Our German comrades are very proud of the decisiveness and combat spirit of our legionnaires.

From issue 6 of Avanguardia, April 22, 1944.

Operational Zone

More than four weeks have passed since the first volunteers of the young Italian SS Legion have reached the front line alongside their comrades from the German SS, to make their contribution, to cancel the shame put upon them by the betrayal of the King and Badoglio and to regain the liberty for the homeland. They have been hard weeks, with freezing nights, rain and mud. Today the sun is shining and springtime is flowering around us. It is Sunday, a day like any other at the front, and everyone is aware of it. All is quiet at the front, not even a shot can be heard and only a few aviators are making curves in the infinite blue background of the sky. The metallic outlines of the planes shine in the sun. We are next to an old house, behind which rise the Alban hills, hills with their cultivated terraces and groves of olive trees, dotted with small mountain towns that are so characteristically necessary for this landscape. A unit of Germans and Italians, wearing helmets and combat gear, is drawn up on parade.

Five Italian SS volunteers awarded the Iron Cross Second Class by *SS-Obf.* Diebitsch in early May. From the left, *Ustuf.* Massimo Flick, *Uscha.* Oceanico Fiaschi, *Uscha.* Giovanni Grandi, *Uscha.* Pietro Orlandoni and legionnaire Ermenegildo Mascitti. (*De Palma*).

Karl Diebitsch.

The allies stand across from each other and between them a small group of five Italian volunteers from the Italian SS legion are just as they have come from their trenches. They are the legionnaires who distinguished themselves by particular courage and who now are being awarded with the Iron Cross for their actions. The commander of a German regiment in whose sector the Italian legionnaires were engaged has just arrived with his officers. Quick, sharp commands, the German and Italian honor guards present arms, the battalion commander presents the force and we pass in review. The commander, with military brevity, speaks to underline the solemnity of the moment. It is the first time that the Iron Cross, this magnificent military

in World War Two 1939-1945

Ermenegildo Mascitti, awarded both classes of the Iron Cross. (*Saronno private collection*)

German soldiers on the Anzio front. (NA)

order, is bestowed upon volunteers of the Italian SS Legion. Faithful to their oath, these men fought. Enemy fire made them tougher and stronger, and in action, they gained the esteem and recognition of their German comrades. The red, white and black ribbon of the most beautiful military award shines with its vivid colors and the black cross with its silver border sparkles in the rays of the sun. But the eyes of the soldiers upon whose chests the decoration is hung sparkle just as well. They are five men for whom this day of honor on the Nettuno front will remain unforgettable: a young second lieutenant – who by quick initiative and decision threw an enemy assault group from its position – two NCOs with strong, lean faces who distinguished themselves in several patrol actions, a boy of 17 years, a Balilla, who from the first day, almost every night, went out on patrol and gathered important information, and finally another young legionnaire, wounded and just released from hospital. He trembles with emotion when the Iron Cross is hung on his chest and his eyes sparkle with joy. A *'Sieg Heil'* (Victory!) addressed to the Führer, the Supreme Commander of the German Armed Forces, concludes the brief ceremony. In this hour, once again the call is raised to the Italian people of all regions of Italy, once again the cry of faith is raised which must reach all active forces, because once again we have shown that the sons of Italy fight and wish to fight and do not want to remain behind and away from their German comrades. Here on the line are the legionnaires of the Italian SS, proud and happy. They lie in the field hospital peaceful and patient and anxiously await the day when they can return to the line alongside their comrades, for fresh battles and new victories. Once again: these men who wear the Iron Cross are not seeking recognition, they simply say: *'We know that we have not done much, we only did our duty. But we will do better, because there is still much to do'.*

From issue 10 of the newspaper Avanguardia dated 20 May 1944.

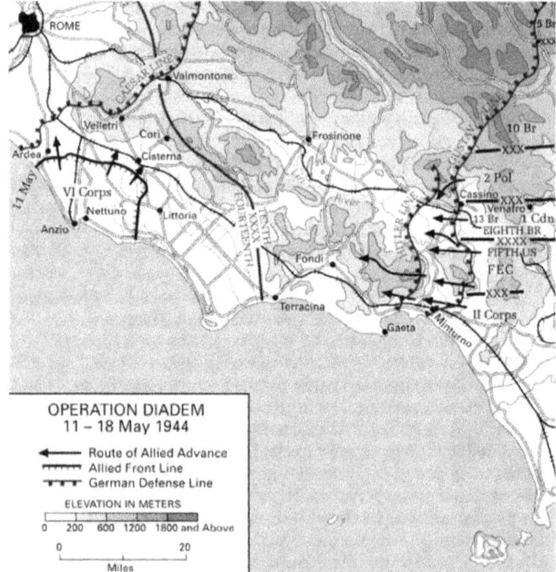

US Army Center of Military History CMH Pub 72-20

And now they go back to the trenches, to their foxholes and little strongholds on the front line, they go back to their comrades, as examples, and I know that soon we will see others come here to receive, as these men have, recognition for their valor. *SS-Oberführer* Kark Diebitsch

The Allied offensive

On May 2, 1944, the Allies launched a major offensive against Montecassino and the Gustav line (Operation *Diadem*) along with a contemporaneous attack by their forces against the bridgehead at Anzio, with the aim of surrounding and wiping out the German *10.Armee*. With the fall of Cassino, after a week of horrific fighting, the American forces began a push against the German forces in the Cisterna area, beginning on May 23. The Italian SS defensive positions were particularly hard hit by the American attack.

US soldiers prepare to cross the Mussolini Canal during the first phase of the offensive.

German half-tracks engaged in defensive combat during Operation Diadem, May 1944.

American Sherman tanks destroyed on the Lazio front.

The Italian legionnaires, hunkered down in their foxholes and trenches, sought to hold out against the assaults by enemy infantry. Antitank defense was provided mainly by *Panzerfaust*. The fighting was carried out in a climate of great confusion with heavy losses on both sides. The American attack fell heavily upon the positions of *3.Kompanie,* which was almost completely wiped out during the fighting. On the same evening of the 23rd, the Americans had reached the Via Appia. The remnants of the Italian SS companies tried to regroup in an attempt to slow down the enemy advance as much as possible. What remained of *1.Kompanie* was ordered to cover the withdrawal of the other units, taking up positions along the Via Appia and remaining there for the rest of the day of the 24th. *SS-Oberführer* Diebitsch and *Ostubaf.* degli Oddi remained with the company and were the last to leave their positions. The men of *2.Kompanie* were also engaged in covering the withdrawal of other German units, before pulling back to the north, along with the support detachment. *SS-Obf.* Diebitsch managed to reach Tivoli. The other men ended up attaching themselves to various German units during the course of their withdrawal to the north. In Florence a march headquarters was set up to collect all of the surviving legionnaires and then to convoy them to Pinerolo; of the 950 legionnaires engaged on the southern front, only two hundred reached the Piedmontese city. The survivors were awarded 22 Iron Crosses Second Class and 52 field promotions from the Germans; Mussolini awarded ten

Young SS volunteer of the *Debica*.

Silver Medals plus the medal for the battalion's standard. In addition, by an order that was rendered official only on September 7, 1944, volunteers who had fought at the front were allowed to wear the black SS collar tabs in lieu of the red tabs. Finally, for all Italian SS volunteers the rank terminology in use by the *Waffen-SS* was introduced. As of April 27, 1944, the Italian Assault Brigade officially became the Italian SS Grenadier Brigade (*Waffen Grenadier Brigade der SS*).

The Debica on the southern front

On April 12, 1944, *SS-Bataillon Debica*, after having been motorized with 32 new Fiat 626 trucks and 12 motorcycles, was transferred to central Italy, to be attached to *Kampfgruppe Diebitsch*. The *Debica* was not sent to the Anzio front immediately, but went to Spoleto to be employed in anti-partisan actions along the Via Flaminia; the Germans were preparing to pull back to the north. Between April and May, *Debica* fought against partisan forces in the area around Nocera Umbra, Assisi and San Severino Marche, losing fifty men between killed, wounded and missing. With the arrival of fresh volunteers, the strength of the battalion reached around five hundred men and twenty officers. On May 31, the battalion was moved to the Tyrrhenian coast to be employed in an anti-landing role, south of Ladispoli and subordinate to *92.Infanterie-Division*, which had just arrived from France. Following the rapid advance of Allied troops, on June 4, 1944 the order was given to withdraw to the north, towards Grosseto. The confusion of the moment led to the unit splitting up into various groups which independently began to pull back to the north. The order, however, did not reach *1.Kompanie* under *Hstuf.* Cantarella, which between June 5 and 6 found itself fighting against units of the US 36th Infantry Division near Palo Laziale, along with a battalion of *92.Infanterie-Division*.

Particularly distinguishing himself in the fighting was the 1st Platoon led by *Oscha.* Walter Morini, which several times risked being surrounded by the Americans. The survivors were able finally to attach themselves to a German battalion and also pull back to Grosseto. On June 16, the roughly two hundred remaining men of the *Debica* were collected in Florence for employment along the Gothic Line, which was under construction.

Bibliography

Massimiliano Afiero, "*Italiani nella Waffen-SS*", Associazione Culturale Ritterkreuz

Massimiliano Afiero, "*The 29th Waffen-SS Grenadier Division 'Italienische Nr.1' and Italians in other units of the Waffen-SS*", Schiffer Publishing

S. Corbatti, M. Nava, "*Sentire-Pensare-Volere: Storia della Legione SS italiana*", Edizioni Ritter

The Polizei-Division on the Leningrad Front – 1942-1943

By Massimiliano Afiero

The Leningrad front, Summer 1942.

Generalleutnant Alfred Wünnenberg.

In late June 1942, the *SS-Polizei-Division* was detached from *I.Armee-Korps*, returning under control of *L.Armee-Korps* (*General der Infanterie* Herbert von Böckmann), located in the area to the south and east of Kolpino on the Leningrad front. The Soviets were particularly sensitive about defending the city of Kolpino; situated only twenty kilometers southeast of Leningrad and being a major industrial center, the Soviet command had transformed the city into a true and proper fortress. With the transfer of the *Polizei-Division* units to new positions in early July, division headquarters were set up in Nikolskoye, while the regiments were positioned as follows: Freitag's *Polizei-Schützen-Regiment 2* was on the left, Borchert's *Pol.Sch.Rgt.3* was in the center and Gieseke's *Pol.Sch.Rgt.1* was on the right. In reserve were the remnants of *Polizei-Aufklärungs-Abteilung* at Badajev, northwest of Nikolskoye. Since July 17, 1942, *SS-Gruf. und Generalleutnant der Polizei* Alfred Wünnenberg had reassumed command of the division. During its first week in the Kolpino sector, there were no noteworthy actions, but only long-range duels between the opposing artillery. On July 23, the first real Soviet attack was made against the *121.Inf.Div.* positions to the left of the *Polizei* positions; the enemy was able to make a dangerous breakthrough at Putrelowo, using armored forces, threatening the German main line of resistance. To ward off the danger to the left flank, it became necessary to destroy the bridge over the Ishora. The mission was assigned to

2./Pol.Pi.Btl., which worked during the night between July 24 and 25, destroying the bridge. To better cover the left flank, which was considered to be to exposed to possible enemy action, a *panzerjäger* platoon was sent to occupy positions in the Krasny Bor area.

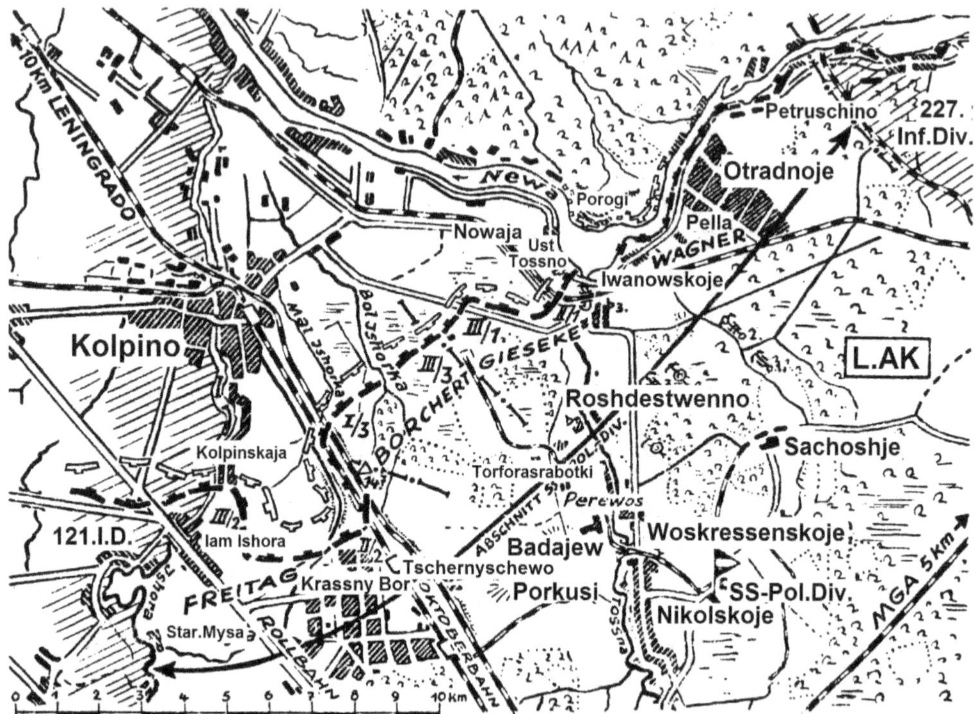

Location of *Polizei-Division* units on the Kolpino front, Summer 1942.

Move of *Polizei* units in the Kolpino sector, Summer 1942 (*Charles Trang Collection*).

in World War Two 1939-1945

On that occasion, *1./Pol.Pz.Jäg.Abt.*, commanded by *Hauptmann* Herbert Schuster, destroyed some thirty enemy bunkers. Soon after, the men of *II./Pol.Sch.Rgt.2* also entered into action, attacking and destroying other enemy bunkers, two fortified positions and two Soviet tanks. Another attack by *II./Pol.Sch.Rgt.1* against enemy positions west of Ust Tossno, along the banks of the Newa River, ended well for the *Polizei* soldiers.

While these attacks were under way, the Soviets in turn attacked the sector defended by *III./Pol.Sch.Rgt.2* with a force of about four hundred men, preceded by strong preparatory artillery fire. The Soviet infantry were able to penetrate the German positions, but were quickly pushed back by a counterattack made by elements of *SS-Polizei-Division*. The fighting continued until July 28, along the entire front held by the division. On August 1,1942, the *SS-FHA* issued an order for the reconstitution and motorization of the SS division. Initially, the Sennelager camp was selected as the training area, but shortly after the camp at Debica in Poland was designated. It was the first step in the transformation of the unit into a new formation of *Waffen SS* armored grenadiers. Meanwhile, fighting continued on the Leningrad front. From the western, high bank of the Ishora, the Soviets could observe and check the entire *Polizei* sector, hitting it

A 105 mm *le.FH 18* of the *Polizei*.

with artillery. On August 5, the enemy again attacked the *Pol.Sch.Rgt.2* positions on both siders of the road that led to Leningrad. A new penetration was quickly sealed and eliminated with few losses. On August 7, another attack was repelled, this time with more serious losses, especially to *Polizei-Pionier-Bataillon* and *Pol.Sch.Rgt.2*.

Summer 1942: *SS-Polizei-Division* infantrymen on the Leningrad front.

A *Polizei* motorcyclist with a SS uniform, on a motorcycle with police license plates. The division had been integrated into the *Waffen SS* in February 1942 (*Charles Trang*).

The defense east of Kolpino

During the night between August 15 and 16, 1942, the *11./Pol.Sch.Rgt.3* positions were attacked by large enemy forces, without the usual preparatory artillery fire. Although caught by surprise, the *Polizei* infantry were able to overcome their initial confusion and drove off the attack causing heavy losses to the enemy. On the morning of the 16th, fresh attacks were made against the positions at Bolshoi Ishorka and along the railway line; several enemy

in World War Two 1939-1945

breakthroughs were also eliminated this time thanks to quick action by *Polizei* and army units. In late evening that day, a massive counterattack was made along the railway line to retake the main line of resistance. On August 20, following heavy artillery barrier fire, the Soviets again attacked the *II./Pol.Sch.Rgt.1* positions two times and both times were thrown back after having suffered heavy losses. Stalled in that sector of the front, they resumed the attack with tanks, landing troops on the eastern bank of the Tossna.

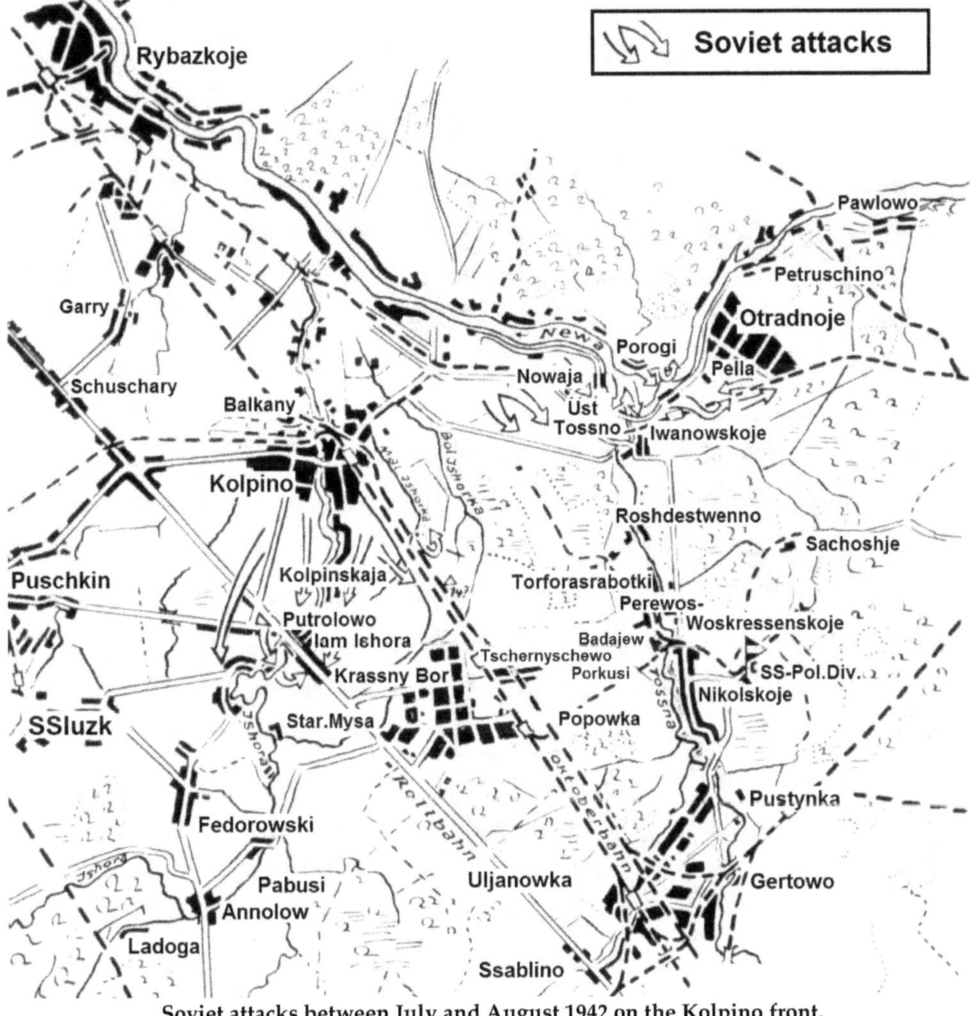

Soviet attacks between July and August 1942 on the Kolpino front.

The enemy made breakthroughs on the right flank of positions held by *II./Pol.Sch.Rgt.1*, but tanks to support fire from the heavy weapons of the regiment's companies *8, 13* and *14*, the attack was repelled. During the fighting, the *6.Kompanie* commander *Hauptmann* Friedrich Karl Jahns was killed. That same day, the Soviet forces that had landed on the eastern bank of the Tossna were heavily shelled by fire from *13./Pol.Sch.Rgt.1*. In the early afternoon, a counterattack by *II./Pol.Sch.Rgt.1* followed, with troops from its headquarters

Soviet artillery on the Leningrad front, Summer 1942.

Soviet tanks destroyed in front of *Polizei* positions.

A German antitank position on the Leningrad front.

and companies *8*, *13* and *14*, managing to throw the Soviet troops back. At the same time, *II./Inf.Rgt.151* attached to *II.Pol.Sch.Rgt.1* committed two companies in a counterattack attempting to recapture the lost positions. In the evening, the western part of the main line of resistance in the *II./Pol.Sch.Rgt.1* sector and along the course of the Neva returned to German hands. A new attack by *5./Infanterie-Regiment 151* infantry was able to wrest other positions along the Neva and the mouth of the Tossna from the Soviets. At that point, the main line of resistance could be considered completely re-established. In order to prevent any further enemy landings across the Tossna, an antitank platoon from *3./Pol.Pz.Jg.Abt.* led by *Leutnant* Max Michel arrived as reinforcement.

Kampfgruppe Schmedding

In order to prevent further enemy landings and to complete the destruction of Soviet forces still present on the eastern bank of the Tossna, a new combat group was formed led by the commander of the *Polizei Panzerjäger Abteilung*, *Oberstleutnant* Ernst Schmedding. *Kampfgruppe Schmedding* was ordered to attack from the south and the north along the Woskrenskoye-Iwanskoye road and to clear the eastern bank of the Tossna. The *Kampfgruppe* consisted of a reinforced infantry company from *II./Infanterie-Regiment 151*, an antitank platoon from *SS-Polizei-Division*, the *4./Sicherungs-Bataillon 636*, other scattered elements of *Sicherungs-Bataillon 636* and the remaining elements of *II./Pz.Rgt.29* (seven tanks). The *Kampfgruppe* moved shortly after noon, reaching the '*Kirov*' railway line in the evening, where it was stopped by a violent enemy attack to the south. With the few forces available, *Oberstleutnant* Schmedding was forced to order his men to dig in on the spot,

in World War Two 1939-1945

unable to move further forward. With the arrival of other forces, mainly of *Panzergrenadier-Regiment 25* led by *Oberst* Bayer, a new *Kampfgruppe* was formed which included the men of *Kampfgruppe Schmedding*. The new *Kampfgruppe Bayer* was to wipe out enemy forces that had crossed the Neva at Ivanovskoye.

A defensive position of *Polizei-Division* on the Neva front, with a 5 cm mortar. Above it, the hulk of a knocked out Soviet KV-1 tank. (*Michael Cremin*).

An artillery observer.

Oberstleutnant Josef Rüschoff of *I./Pol.Art.Rgt.* was assigned to the combat group as a liaison officer to coordinate artillery support. At the same time, the division ordered *Pol.Sch.Rgt.1* to continue to hold the main line of resistance and to prevent any further attempts to land on the western bank of the Tossna. To that end, *Flak* batteries and antitank guns were to be emplaced at the mouth of the river to deal with any Soviet armed barges and other naval transport vessels. During the night between 20 and 21 August, two KV-1 heavy tanks were knocked out at short range by *Leutnant* Michel's antitank platoon. While *Kampfgruppe Bayer* was preparing to attack the enemy positions, the Soviets attacked in *Major* Karl

Schümers' *II./Pol.Sch.Rgt.1* sector. After the usual preliminary artillery bombardment along the entire defensive front, an attack followed by Soviet infantry supported by four tanks in the sector between the Neva and the 'Kirovgrad' railway line.

Left, *SS-Polizei-Division* NCOs in a trench on the Kolpino front. Right, German infantry ready to go on the attack, Summer 1942.

A 20mm *Flak* position on the Leningrad front, Summer 1942.

Two enemy tanks were quickly knocked out. During a follow-on attack, the Soviets were able to break into the right wing in the *II./Inf.Rgt.151* sector. An immediate counterattack was necessary to re-establish the situation; in that action, the soldiers of *6./Pol.Sch.Rgt.1* distinguished themselves. In the eastern sector of *Pol.Sch.Rgt.1*, *Kampfgruppe Bayer* was

A 37mm antitank gun in action against soviet tanks.

August 1942, Leningrad front: Hulks of Soviet tanks knocked out in front of *SS-Polizei-Division* positions.

A *Nebelwerfer* rocket launcher supporting *SS-Pol.Art.Rgt.*

ready to launch an attack with two battalions, moving from east to west. Strong resistance put up by Soviet troops made it necessary to call in more forcers, namely *II./Geb.Rgt.100* under *Major* Pfeiffer. The mouth of the Tossna was thus reached, but a fresh surprise enemy attack stalled any further forward progress.

Operation Nordlicht

On August 21, 1942, *Feldmarschall* von Manstein reached the Uschaki area with the staffs of *XXX* and *LIV.Armee-Korps* to discuss the new *Führer* directive number 45. It called for *Heeresgruppe Nord* to conquer Leningrad by early September; the operation was codenamed *Feuerzauber*, that is, 'Magic Fire'. For this task, five divisions of *11,Armee*, supported by heavy and super-heavy artillery, were to be added to reinforce the sector. A week later, the operation was renamed *Nordlicht* (Northern Light) The influx of these new forces did not however take place in a timely manner. Only elements of *132.Infanterie-Division* joined the units of *3.Gebirgs-Division* already in place. The heavy artillery coming from the Crimean front remained hidden for weeks, in great secrecy. In the *Pol.Sch.Rgt.1* sector, the *I./Gebirgsjäger-Rgt.* of *5.Gebirgs-Division*, led by Major Wecker, was supposed to arrive as reinforcement. But before that happened, on August 22, the Soviets attacked in that very sector and in particular against the positions held by *II./Pol.Sch.Rgt.1*. The enemy penetrated in the *5.Kompanie* sector, on the left wing of the battalion's defensive front. As soon as the *Gebirgsjäger* troops reached the area, they were sent to close the open gap and were then soon after thrown into a counterattack along with the *5. And 7.Kompanie* of *II./Pol.Sch.Rgt.1*.

Location of units on the Leningrad front, late August 1942.

A German 105 mm howitzer on the Leningrad front, 1942.

The Soviet attack also hit the right flank of *III./Pol.Sch.Rgt.1* with many enemy units that were pushing along the Tossna towards the south. The battalion command post came under attack; the situation was stabilized thanks to providential fire support by several artillery batteries. During the night between August 22 and 23, the Soviets again attempted o land forces to the east of the mouth of the Tossna, taking heavy losses. In the early afternoon of the 23rd, another Soviet attack west of the river's mouth against *Pol.Sch.Rgt.1* positions; the *Polizei* infantrymen fended off the threat inflicting heavy losses on the enemy. With the coming of night, the Soviets attacked again, achieving numerous breakthroughs and heavily engaging the *Polizei* soldiers, who had to fight tenaciously to close off all of the gaps made in the defensive front. These continuous attacks and counterattacks lasted until August 27, when the Soviets unleashed another offensive in the Gaitolowo area with their 2nd Shock

Army, giving rise to what would be known in history as the first battle of Lake Ladoga. According to the report written by *SS-Staf.* Otto Gieseke, commander of *Pol.Sch.Rgt.1,* Soviet losses in the fighting between August 19 and 25, were at least 15,000 men killed or wounded, in addition to about thirty tanks destroyed.

Soviet infantry going on the attack.

An *MG 34* in firing position, Summer 1942.

***SS-Stubaf.* Karl Schümers.**

The Knight's Cross for Karl Schümers

SS-Stubaf. Karl Schümers, previously awarded the German Cross in Gold on August 3, 1942, was also proposed for the Knight's Cross (officially conferred on 30 September 1942) by his regimental commander, *SS-Staf.* Otto Gieseke. Following is the text of the proposal: '...*In the period between 19 and 26 August 1942, the Soviets attempted to break the defensive ring around Leningrad by continuous attacks focused on the mouth of the Tossna River. These attacks were supported by landings of troops crossing the River Neva, with the aim of first capturing the road and the railway bridge at the mouth of the Tossna and then to push along the railway line to Mga. There, there was to be a linkup with enemy elements that were attacking to the west, thus liberating Leningrad. The attack was made by numerous infantry forces supported by tanks, dive bombers,*

SS-Stubaf. Gieseke with other officers, Summer 1942.

An MG 34 on a heavy mount, Summer 1942.

warships and artillery batteries of all calibers. The expenditure of artillery ammunition was comparable to that of the great battles of 1914-1918. At the center of this furious defensive battle was II./SS-Pol.Schtz.Rgt.1, *under the energetic command of Major Schümers. He had already distinguished himself by his personal courage and excellent tactical leadership of his battalion, not only on the occasion of the early phases of the campaign on the Eastern Front, but in particular with the* Polizei-Division *during the bitter winter battles on the Volchov River. After the landing of enemy forces near the mouth of the Tossna, under cover of numerous warships, the Soviets were able to penetrate the right wing of* II.Bataillon *on August 19, 1942. They advanced as far as the Tossna, north of the road bridge. Major Schümers immediately grasped the seriousness of the situation and while the enemy continued on to the south, he turned the flank of his battalion and defended both bridges. He went to the area of the breakthrough with some of the men of his staff and gathered up*

the surviving elements of his company on the right flank. He then made a hasty counterattack with a movement on the flanks. During the furious close-quarter fighting most of the enemy forces were wiped out and the rest thrown back. The main combat line thus returned into the hands of the battalion. Following a massive artillery barrage and with tank and air support, on August 23, 1942 two to three enemy regiments were able to break into the main combat line near the road bridge. The Soviet soldiers pushed towards the Tossna and got as far as the battalion's position along the 'Kirov' railway line. The bridge, one of the two critical crossings over the river, ended up in enemy hands. Sensing this new serious threat, once again Major Schümers immediately took the initiative. After having sent forward the two companies of young recruits who had just arrived from the fatherland, he collected the remaining personnel of his company on the flank and personally led a counterattack with these men. Thanks to his determination and his resoluteness, Major Schümers was able to vanquish the Soviets during this furious close-quarter fighting. The bulk of the enemy force was wiped out and the survivors fled in panic. The road and the bridge were again in the hands of the battalion. Major Schümers quickly began to reconstitute the main combat line, repelling the Soviet attacks that followed and inflicting heavy losses.

Polizei-Division awardees of the Iron Cross Second Class (*Michael Cremin Collection*).

A *Polizei* defensive position on the Leningrad front, 1942.

Twice, new enemy incursions were eliminated by courageous counterattacks thanks to Major Schümers' determination and leadership. In addition, the enemy lost control of the road and rail

A Spanish volunteer of the *Division Azul*.

A Soviet machine gun in position, 1942.

bridges across the river, vital for his advance towards Mga, making his attempts to liberate Leningrad in vain. The bulk of two Soviet rifle divisions, several regiments and independent battalions, thirty tanks, many transport barges and several assault craft were destroyed during the fighting…'.

Resuming operations

In early August 1942, the *SS-FHA* decided to reconstitute the third battalion of each of the division's regiments; on 26 August, with a further order, it was also decided to motorize them. Beginning on September 2, some officers and NCOs were sent to the camp at Debica to organize the new battalions. On September 4, 1942, von Manstein's *11.Armee* assumed command of military operations against Leningrad. The *XXVI* and *L.Armee-Korps* were thus subordinated to him. At the same time, *XXX* and *LIV.Armee-Korps* were inserted between the *XXVI* and *L.Armee-Korps*. During the night between September 5 and 6, the *SS-Polizei-Division* and *121.Infanterie-Division* were subordinated to *LIV.Armee-Korps*. The Ishora River continued to mark the boundary between the operational sectors of the two units. On September 6, *SS-Polizei-Division* successfully repulsed several enemy attacks in the sectors held by the 1st and 3rd regiments. On September 7, a new attack in the *III./Pol.Sch.Rgt.1* sector resulted in several enemy penetrations, a situation that led to intervention by reinforcements to stave off the threat. That same day, *121.Infanterie-Division* was relieved by the Spanish *250.Infanterie-Division*, whose units occupied the front to the south of Kolpino, between Krasny Bor and Puschkin. With the integration of the *'Blau Division'* into the defensive scheme

in World War Two 1939-1945

SS-Stubaf. **Wilhelm Dietrich.**

Capturing Soviet prisoners during the fighting.

of *LIV.Armee-Korps*, the left boundary of *SS-Polizei-Division* was shifted further to the right, that is, to the east.

The Knight's Cross for Wilhelm Dietrich

In this latest fighting, the commander in the field *of III./Pol.Sch.Rgt.1, Hauptmann* Wilhelm Dietrich distinguished himself, and who based on the proposal by *Oberst* Otto Gieseke, was awarded the Knight's Cross on 15 October 1942. Following is the text of the proposal: '..*Following the tough defensive fighting in the Neva sector, between August 19 and 25, 1942,* II.Bataillon, *which until that time had been in the thick of the fighting, was relieved by* III./Polizei-Schützen-Regiment 1, *commanded by* Hauptmann *Wilhelm* Dietrich.

On August 30, after a brief pause, the enemy again attempted to break into our lines. In the days that followed, the enemy attacked the III./Polizei-Schützen-Regiment 1 *positions, supported by tanks, bombers and fighters. It was also supported by massive artillery fire of all calibers, which was reminiscent of the enormous expenditure of ammunition during the First World War. The objectives of the enemy attacks were to capture the road and rail bridges across the northern Tossna, and then to push towards Mga and relieve Leningrad. Many enemy attacks supported by tanks were driven off, with heavy losses to the Soviets, who were engaged in furious close-quarter combat. The enemy, with tank support, was able to break into the western positions of* III./Polizei-Schützen-Regiment 1 *in the early hours of 4 September 1942 and at the same time, throwing in strong reserves, penetrated the main combat line.* Hauptmann *Dietrich immediately recognized the critical situation and above all the danger that his battalion could be completely annihilated. A first counterattack failed because of strong enemy resistance and enemy tank fire. Telephone communications were cut and it was not possible to call for reinforcements or artillery support. Despite the intense Katyusha and artillery fire,* Hauptmann *Dietrich was finally able to go personally to the area of the enemy incursion with a handful of men from his staff. At the same time, he ordered elements of III./Infanterie-Regiment 435 to assume defensive positions along the Kirov railway line, to impede at all costs the enemy from continuing on to the south. After* Hauptmann *Dietrich succeeded in gathering together many stragglers, he quickly mounted a counterattack with these men and part of 10.Kompanie. during the close-quarter fighting, fought mainly with hand grenades and bayonets. The Soviets were thrown back and the area of the incursion was liberated.*

SS defensive position with an *MG 34* **on a heavy tripod.**

German officers on the front line, 1942.

The enemy attacks continued. The next day, September 5, 1942, the Soviets, with tank and artillery support, managed to penetrate the left wing of III./SS-Polizei-Schützen-Regiment 1. All of the officers in the area of the incursion were either wounded or killed and their units broke up. A gap of about three hundred meters was opened between II. and III.Bataillon. Ther were no reserves and it was not possible to pull the men back to new positions. The Soviets sensed a great opportunity and continued their attacks. Some enemy troops had already gotten behind the right wing of II.Bataillon, which was spread out along the Kirov railway line. While the Soviets had thrown in fresh forces, the right wing of the regiment was about to collapse. Counterattacks were repulsed by strong enemy resistance. It was then that Hauptmann *Dietrich, with extreme resolve, took drastic measures.*

SS-Staf. Otto Gieseke.

SS-Hstuf. Helmut Ringholz.

Wirth the rest of the battalion he had at hand he was able to make it to the Kirov railway line after tough close-quarter fighting under constant enemy fire. After having overrun strong enemy forces, he was able to seal the breach and to re-establish contact with II.Bataillon, *restoring the main combat line. The defensive success achieved in these days against enemy attacks, especially the critical tactical situation between September 4 and 5 1942, were mainly due to the personal courage and determination of* Hauptmann *Dietrich. Almost all of the machine guns and rifles had been rendered inoperable by the enemy's intense barrier fire. Most of the mortars had been buried. Hand grenades and bayonets were the only weapons still available. During the incessant fighting, heavy losses were inflicted on the enemy, at least 10,000 men, in a very constricted area. At least thirteen enemy tanks were destroyed or immobilized.*

Success was due mainly to the heroic efforts of Hauptmann *Dietrich and his men, who fought strenuously following their commander's example. The vast offensive and the last enemy attempt to capture the railway bridge over the Tossna to lay down the base for a relief action for Leningrad were thus cancelled. The enemy suffered heavy losses of men and equipment…'.*

Other awards

On September 24, by divisional order number 31, award of the German Cross in Gold was announced for *SS-Staf.* Gieseke (officially conferred on 12 September 1942), commander of *SS-Pol.Sch.Rgt.1*, followed on September 30, 1942 by award of the Knight's Cross, based on the proposal by the division commander, Alfred Wünnenberg, for having distinguished himself while leading his men in the latest fighting. Also awarded the German Cross in Gold on September 16, 1942 were *Hauptmann* Egon Neuss, commander of *III./Pol.Sch.Rgt.1* and *Oberfeldwebel* Karl Labahn, a platoon leader in *5./SS-Pol.Inf.Rgt.2.* Labahn had particularly distinguished himself in action in the Kolpino sector in late July 1942, during which many enemy positions were destroyed. While returning to his position, Labahn tripped a mine, losing his right foot. After having been relieved of front-line duty because of the serious injury, thanks to his front-line experience, he was assigned as a company commander of *7./SS-Pz.Gr.Ausb.-u.Ers.Btl.4* in 1944. On September 25, 1942, *SS-Hstuf.* Helmut Ringholz, commander of *7./Pol.Schtz.Rgt.1*, was awarded the German Cross in Gold, based on the recommendation by his battalion commander, Karl Schümers. Following is an extract from the recommendation: '*...On August 22, 1942, during the Soviet penetration into our main combat line near the bend of the Neva, on his own initiative* Hauptmann *Ringholz formed an assault group. Fighting at the head of this group with hand grenades and a machine pistol, they reached the trenches of the nearby sector. On August 23, 1942, the Soviets were again able to break into our main combat line. Once again,* Hauptmann *Ringholz, on his initiative and with great energy, intercepted the enemy forces and threw them back.*

Autumn 1942: *SS-Polizei-Division* soldiers sheltering from the rain using *zeltbahnen*.

Attack by Soviet Infantry and tanks, 1942.

This prevented any further enemy advance. During this fighting, Hauptmann *Ringholz was seriously wounded in the chest by rifle fire...*'. This serious wound kept Ringholz confined to bed for a long period and he was unable to return to the front. He was then assigned to the German police offices in Plauen.

The new winter campaign

In concert with the encirclement of soviet forces of the 2nd Shock Army in the area northeast of Mga, the *SS-Polizei-Division* was engaged in impeding a relief attack made by fully eight enemy divisions in the area east of Kolpino. On September 25, *Generalfeldmarschall* von Manstein ordered the annihilation of the surrounded Soviet forces; *SS-Polizei-Division* participated with only its *Flak* batteries.

An 88 mm *Flak* gun of *Polizei-Flak-Abteilung*, Autumn 1942.

***SS-Gruf.* Wünnenberg.**

Having failed in their attempt to lift the siege of Leningrad, the Soviets put off any further offensives until early 1943, so that during October there were only some local attacks which involved *Polizei* units only minimally.

On October 15, the division's three infantry regiments were officially renamed as *SS-Polizei-Infanterie-Regiment*. Later, on 1 February 1943, their designation again changed to *SS-Polizei-Grenadier-Regiment*.

On October 19, the *SS-Polizei-Division* was subordinated to *XXX.Armee-Korps*, while *250.(spanische).Infanterie-Division* remained attached to *LIV.Armee-Korps*.

On October 31, *10./SS-Pol.Inf.Rgt.2* led by *SS-Hstuf.* Wittekind Gärtner, was successfully engaged in an attack against enemy positions as part of a series of offensive actions to stabilize the main line of the front. On 6 November, *LIV.Armee-Korps* assumed control of the *XXX.Armee-Korps* sector, after that corps had been completely pulled out of the front line. With the progressive fall in temperature, the German troops were mainly engaged in building shelters and fortifications for the winter season.

***Polizei* soldiers in front of the hulk of a *KV-1*, Winter 1942-43 (*Charles Trang Collection*).**

A German soldier with two ammo containers on the edge of a village, during an attack. On the left is an assault gun moving ahead.

Between late November and Early December, the Soviets carried out a series of local exploratory attacks. On November 30, *10./Pol.Inf.Rgt.1*, commanded by *SS-Hstuf.* Erwin Menzel, conducted a successful attack against enemy positions. On December 4, another attack was successfully made by *5./Pol.Inf.Rgt.2*, under the temporary command of *SS-Ustuf.* Martin Harnack.

On December 14, men of the *SS-Polizei-Aufkl.-Abteilung* were engaged in the *SS-Pol.Inf.Rgt.3* sector in an attack against enemy positions along the railway line. Thanks to the ability of *SS-Hstuf.* Otto Prager, the recon battalion commander, both assault groups that took part in the action were able to break through the enemy lines under covering fire from heavy weapons. Many Soviet positions were destroyed, among which a heavily

SS-*Stubaf*. Otto Prager.

fortified position from which the enemy controlled all of the surrounding area. The two assault groups, led by *Unteroffizier* Dorschner and *Obergefreiter* Nuhn, ended up destroying six enemy bunkers, the fortified positions, another seven fire positions and a great quantity of arms and munitions. The entire operation was supported by elements of *13./SS-Pol.Inf.Rgt.3*, by *II./SS-Pol.Art.Rgt.* and two batteries of *250.(spanische) Infanterie-Division*. Prager's action was reported in the proposal written by *SS-Brigdf.* Fritz Schmedes, who recommended him for the German Cross in Gold, and which he was awarded officially on November 14, 1944: '...*On December 14, 1942, an assault group of* SS-Pol.Aufkl.Abt. *commanded at the time by* SS-Hstuf. *Prager, went into action to clear out a very wide sector in front of Leningrad, where an enemy bridgehead had formed since October. Elimination of this prominent Soviet bridgehead had a particular tactical significance for the entire sector of the front, because it put the right flank of our forces in great danger.* SS-Hstuf. *Prager's action had been in the making for several days. The plans against the enemy had to be studied with great attention because for our positions, capture of the ground held by the enemy meant shifting the main line of the front (*HKL, HauptKampfLinie*) to the south by four kilometers.* Hstuf. *Prager undertook the action by personally and with precision carrying out the task assigned to him, destroying the enemy position that threatened us, in just twelve minutes. The enemy was then pursued and sustained heavy losses. Elimination of the bridgehead from which several enemy attacks had emanated had been studied in the smallest details and was completed with exemplary tactical success by* Hstuf. *Prager. This led to significant easing of pressure on our troops in that sector of the front.* SS-Hstuf. *Prager's action was appreciated by the* Wehrmacht *as well, which mentioned it in its bulletin. The enemy suffered heavy losses in men and equipment compared to our scarce losses, precisely: six bunkers occupied, four bunkers full of equipment, one sniper position and eight combat positions. Large quantities of ammunition were captured, which were destroyed. The enemy left fifty dead on the field, among which was a company commander.*'.

On December 15, a new offensive was made by *III./SS-Pol.Inf.Rgt.1*, led by *SS-Hstuf.* Hans Traupe, which was also crowned with complete success for the men of the *Polizei*. The following days saw other offensive actions with mixed results.

Bibliography

Massimiliano Afiero, "*4.SS-Polizei-Panzergrenadier-Division*", Associazione Culturale Ritterkreuz
Massimiliano Afiero, "*The 4th Waffen-SS Panzergrenadier Division 'Polizei'*", Schiffer Publishing
Friedrich Husemann, "*Die guten Glaubens waren. Geschichte der SS-Polizei-Division (4. SS-Panzergrenadier-Division). Band II: 1943 – 1945*", Munin-Verlag, Osnabrück 1973

La Croix de Guerre Légionnaire
by Rene Chavez

Picture above shows a much-publicized ceremony during which some *"Croix de Guerre Légionnaire"* were awarded to LVF soldiers for the second anniversary of the creation of the unit at the Court of the Invalides, Paris, August 27, 1943.

The *"Croix de Guerre Légionnaire"* (War Cross Legionnaire) or often known improperly by the collecting circles as the *"Légion des Voluntaires Français"* (LVF) Cross was a decoration originally intended to be awarded to members of the "Légion Tricolore" (Tricolor Legion). But because of the short lived formation of the Légion Tricolore (officially created on 28 June 1942 and dissolved on the 28 December 1942) and the fact that members of the legion never actually fought combat in the Eastern Front, the award was for all intense purposes given to LVF veterans, as well as to soldiers of the short lived *"Phalange Africaine"* (African phalanx). For simplicity sake the cross is going to be mention in this article as the LVF

Cross. Before we talked about the LVF Cross I am providing a very short brief history of the formation of the LVF, Légion Tricolore and Phalange Africaine.

The Légion des Volontaires Français contre le Bolchevisme (LVF)

When Germany invaded Russia in June 1941 it caused great excitement among the collaborating political parties and para-military home based formations in western Europe. They now found a new unity in their desire to participate in the Russian campaign. In France, the collaborating political parties of the occupied zone announced the creation of the *"Légion des Voluntaires Français contre le Bolshevisme (LVF)"* during a massive meeting at the Vélodrome d'Hiver in Paris on July 18, 1941. Initially the Vichy Government had enacted a law that forbade Frenchmen from enlisting into "foreign armies" to prevent them from joining with the Free French forces of exiled General Charles de Gaulle. Since the LVF was a private affair officially created on August 5, Marshal Petain amended the law so that no objection would be raised for Frenchmen enlisting into the LVF. The first recruiting center was opened at 12 rue Auber, Paris. Additional recruiting centers where placed in the occupied zone, and later all over France. From July 1941 up to June 1944, a total of 6500 Frenchmen were selected into the LVF, but the unit never had more of 2500 soldiers on the frontline. These volunteers were placed in the Borgnis-Desbordes barracks at Versailles. They wore standard German army uniforms and had the French national arm shield inscribed "FRANCE" placed on their right sleeve.

Colonel Roger Labonne.

German made BeVo shield.

French Colonel Roger Labonne assumed command of the legion. On September 4, the first draft of volunteers of 828 officers and men left to the *"Truppenuebungsplatz Deba"* (troop exercise area Deba), located in Poland. On September 20, the second Legion contingent of 896 men was sent to Deba troop training barracks. By October 1941, the LVF was up to strength of two battalions with 181 Officers and 2271 other ranks with a liaison staff of 35 Germans. The LVF was registered as *"Franzosischer Infanterie Regiment 638"* (638th Infantry

LVF soldiers in the Eastern Front. A German General is presenting a military award to a French officer.

LVF soldiers marching in the cold winter, Eastern Front.

LVF soldiers on the Eastern Front, November 1941.

Regiment) of the German Army. By the end of October both battalions proceeded by rail to Smolensk and then by truck and on foot towards the front line near Moscow. The LVF joined the German 7th Infantry Division near Golowkovo. In early December a 3rd battalion of 1400 other recruits of the LVF was sent to Deba troop training barracks. Badly trained and already exhausted, the legion fought in early December 1941 and suffered heavy casualties. In February 1942, the 1st and 2nd battalions of the LVF were caught up in the Soviet winter counter-offensive. During this winter offensive, the 2nd battalion was over-run by Soviet forces near Djunovo and virtually annihilated. The LVF lost half of its strength either through enemy action or by frostbite. In March 1942, Colonel Labonne was recalled to Paris and relieved of his command. A new training period started, and the "new" legion saw the "political victory" of the P.P.F. (Parti populaire français) of Jacques Doriot, who massively infiltrated the unit. The LVF was pulled out of the front line and for 18 months it operated as two separate battalions. The first battalion was placed under the command of Major Lacroix and the third battalion under Major Demessine. During the summer of 1942 the 1st battalion subordinated to the 186th German Security Division, which was deployed in anti-partisan activities near Smolensk. The 3rd battalion was in the southwestern part of Smolensk and fought anti-partisans near Volost where it suffered heavy casualties.

in World War Two 1939-1945

La Légion Tricolore

On June 28, 1942, the LVF was renamed as the Légion Tricolore. It was financed by the Vichy government, and headed by Raymond Lachal, Pierre Laval's right-hand man. Jacques Benoist-Méchin was the principle architect of the creation of the Légion Tricolore[1]. Volunteers would wear French uniforms and served to protect French interest. It was quietly dissolved after only 6 months in existence. Hitler didn't approve the Legion on transferring into a French governing system and ordered to be disbanded on 28 December 1942. Former members of the Légion Tricolore were allowed to rejoin the LVF. By February 1943, the Vichy Government, through Law no. 95, finally recognized the LVF as an official military organization. In June 1943, after active recruiting and reorganizing, the LVF was refitted and prepared to serve under the German 186th Security Division at Smolensk.

La Phalange Africaine

The Phalange Africaine is a unit created in November 1942 by the Vichy Government in response to the landing of the Allies in French Morocco and Algeria. On November 14, 1942, the idea of an African Phalange is approved in Paris with the support of the French Vichy Government and German military authorities. The Phalange Africaine consisted of about 350 or so volunteers, about 2/3 French and 1/3 Algerians and incorporated into the German 2nd Battalion, 754 Pz-Gren Rgt 334 of the 5th Pz-Gren Division. On April 7, 1943 it fought defending the Medjez-El-Bab area against British forces (78th Infantry Division), under command of Captain Dupuis. Because of this

Recruitment poster for the Légion Tricolore.

Captain Dupuis on the *Signal* magazine.

engagement it earned the congratulations of the German General Weber who distributes several LVF crosses as well as German Iron crosses. 9 days later, allied forces launch a

The Croix de Guerre.

general offensive on the sector. The Phalange positions are destroyed by artillery and tank support. In one hour, the unit lost half of its men. The remaining survivors retreated to the German positions and the allied forces take the gates of Tunis. In early May 1943 it was renamed *"Légion des Volontaires Français de Tunisie"* (Legion of French Volunteers of Tunisia). Most members went into captivity upon the Axis surrender in Northern Africa in May 1943.

The Croix de Guerre

The Croix de Guerre was originally instituted by law on April 2, 1915 and consists of a cross with two crossed swords and a small disc medallion attached to the center located on the obverse and reverse of the cross. It was the only decoration awarded by France during World War One for valor in the battlefield. It was awarded to individuals of any rank who distinguished themselves by heroism in combat against enemy forces and also to anyone mentioned in dispatches for bravery in action. Subsequent acts of bravery on the part of recipients earned the following:

- Bronze star for those who had been mentioned at the regiment or brigade level.
- Silver star for those who had been mentioned at division level.
- Gold star for those who had been mentioned at the corps level.
- Bronze palm leaf for those who had been mentioned at the army level.
- Silver palm stands for five bronze ones.
- Silver gold palm for those who had been mentioned at the Free French Forces level (World War II only).

French soldier wearing the LVF cross.

Enlisted soldiers who earned the cross with the "Palme de Bronze" (Bronze Palm) attached to the green and red ribbon, were treated with the greatest of respect. As indicated, the Croix de Guerre could also be awarded to units that distinguished themselves. When World War II broke out in 1939, a new Croix de Guerre was created by the Prime Minister Édouard Daladier. It was then abolished by Vichy Government in 1941, which created their owned version of the "Croix de Guerre 1939-1940." The center medallion was the same as the 1939 version but the reverse the medallion have the

in World War Two 1939-1945

inscription date 1939-1940. The ribbon was completely changed to a green color with five black stripes. Illustrated is the reverse of the Vichy model showing the center medallion with the date 1939-1940 and the new color ribbon. Three other versions with different dates were produced[2]. Also In 1943, General Giraud in Algiers created another version of the Croix de Guerre. Both Vichy and "Giraud Croix de guerre" were abolished by General de Gaulle in 1944[2].

The Croix de Guerre Légionnaire

The LVF cross was created on July 6, 1942[3]. However, it was officially Decree (Article 4) by the head of the Vichy government on 16 September 1942, recognizing the LVF cross as an official award by the Vichy government[4]. Military citations were already being conferred under the conditions laid down by the Statute of the Légion Tricolore to its members, which included the allocation of the LVF Cross[5]. The production and awarding of cross terminated on November 20, 1944.

Croix de Guerre Légionnaire.

The initiative of the creation of the cross was introduced by Jacques Benoist-Méchin who was the Vichy Secretary of State and Chairman of the central Committee of the Légion Tricolore. The realization of the cross was entrusted to a Roland Gaucher (pen name). According to sources such as Dr. Klietmann and Lefévre the manufacturer of the LVF cross was entrusted to the firm "Arthus-Bertrand," however, this has been debated among collectors on who actually manufactured the LVF cross and will be mentioned later on in this article. The LVF cross was formed from parts of the overall 1939 Croix de Guerre model and has a standard width of 38mm. The swords were removed, side metal traces were the sword were removed are normally visible. The swords were substituted by a stylized laurel wreath 25mm outer diameter. Each side of the wreath is made of 12 leaves and is tied by a large ribbon knot. The laurel wreath is die-stamped and is welded to the four arms of the cross around the center. The laurel wreath is obviously a reference to the Napoleonic Empire[6].

The center medallion (circular disc) of the Croix de Guerre was replaced by another medallion of 14mm in diameter that shows the bronze emblem of the French imperial eagle holding four lightning rods in its talons and the French Tricolor shield placed in the center of the eagle's chest. The tricolor shield has the inscription "FRANCE" on top. As indicated the emblem illustrating the eagle was a Napoleonic Imperial symbol. The reverse shows the medallion with the inscription: "CROIX DE GUERRE LEGIONNAIRE."

 in World War Two 1939-1945

The three horizontal characters should have a 1.5mm height measurement. The medallion has a concave shape on both sides and the cross has a golden bronze color. Some of these LVF crosses have been found with markings. These markings are shown on one of the sides of the cross legs and has a hand stamped in-print. The marking normally will have a cornucopia style horn followed by either the letters "BR" or "BP"[7]. The LVF cross shown above has the cornucopia style horn and "BR" marking. These markings found on the cross have been attributed to the firm "Monnaie de Paris" (Paris Mint).

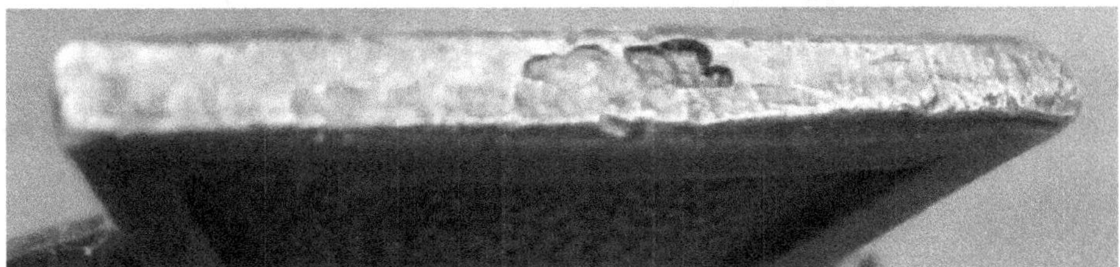

Concerning who made the circular medallions is where the debate is among collectors and historians some said the Monnaie de Paris others indicate "Arthus-Bertrand, Paris (APB)" but no evidence has been found.

The ribbon color was totally different from the official 1939 French sanction ribbons but similar in color to the Vichy cross ribbons. The LVF cross is held by a green ribbon of 37.5mm width showing on each side a wide vertical black edges measuring 4.5mm (late 5mm) with seven vertical black stripes with a width of 0.05mm spaced between 3mm black stripes. The LVF cross was worn on the left side pocket of the uniform. According to Lefévre it has been reported that some legionnaires wore the badge on the chest like the German first class Iron Cross.

LVF Croix de Guerre CITATIONS

The first ceremony of the Croix de Guerre Légionnaire being awarded was held on August 27, 1942, the date was chosen to commemorate the first anniversary of the creation of the LVF. This award ceremony was held at Hotel des Invalides, Paris and attended by various Vichy Government officials among them was General Galy Commissioner-general of the Légion Tricolore. During this ceremony, 110 citations were awarded to LVF veterans wearing German uniforms, which included four Frenchman whom already had earned the German 2nd class Iron Cross: Monsignor de Mayol of Lupe (Chaplain of the Legion), Second Lieutenant Kingsley, Legionnaire Delrieu and Colonel Labonne[8]. Thirty of those awarded posthumously to relatives of legionnaires killed or deceased; ten or so crosses were given to wounded legionnaires who were being treated at the hospital of the Foch in Suresnes Foundation[9]. It should be noted that LVF crosses were available during the award presentation. This is true base on ceremonial pictures of LVF men wearing the LVF cross. The new LVF ribbons (a transitional ribbon) for some reason were not available in time so the LVF crosses were presented with ribbons of the Vichy "Croix de Guerre 1939-1940". In addition, when the army or regiment citations were awarded, the decorations themselves did not have the Palm leaf's or Stars attached to the cross ribbons. On November 24, 1942, Colonel Henriet, Chief of Staff of the Commissioner-General of the Legion and the State Secretary of defense General Bridoux conferred 154 individual citations to members of the LVF:

1) 105 to the order of the army, (Palm in bronze), including a vast majority posthumously.
2) 27-the order of the brigade (bronze star).
3) 22-the order of the regiment (bronze star).

A note from colonel Henriet dated December 24 indicates that 45 new citations of the order have been submitted to the State Secretary of Defense General Bridoux and 38 other proposed citations coming from the 1st office of the general Commissioner of the Legion to the two battalions of the "638th Infantry Regiment". According to the article of Lefévre it states that on March 23, 1943, an announcement by the State Secretary of Defense providing the LVF delegation with a new list of 358 recipients of the award. The 358 qualified recipients were awarded with the following citations:

- 98 Army Citations with the bronze palm leaf.
- 1 citation with the silver star.
- 14 citations with the brigade bronze star
- 245 citations with the regimental bronze star.

These citations were divided between 19 officers, 81 NCOs and 258 enlisted. According to Dr. Klietmann supposedly about 300 LVF crosses were distributed between 1942 and 1944. The cross obviously became prohibited after the war ended and was removed with the Decree of 7 January 1944. Citations of the cross continued to be awarded but there is no indication if LVF crosses were provided(10). This represents less than half of the total citations resulting in the award of the cross. This is supported by the fact that many legionnaires testify having received the citations without the decoration LVF Cross.

Notes

[1] Jacques Benoist-Méchin proposed that La Légion Tricolore take the form of a small French Army with its own logistics and that it would fight in German uniforms, but be authorized to wear the French uniform in the rear.

[2] Croix de Guerre Wikipedia.

[3] Source : Forbes, Robert"Pour L'Europe, page 85....

[4] Official application for the LVF cross was submitted on 18 July 1942.

[5] Source: Lefévre, Eric, La Croix de Guerre Legionnaire, Militaria Magazine.....

[6] The laurel wreath was symbolic representation of the Napoleonic emblem.

[7] These abbreviated letters "BP" stands for "Bronze Patiné" and the abbreviated letter "BR" for "Bronze."

[8] During this ceremony there is no indication base on period pictures that show members of the Légion Tricolore being awarded with military citations. The Légion Tricolore was under the supervision of the French military and they wore French uniforms.

[9] Source Lefévre article.

Bibliography

Eric Lefévre, "*La Croix de Guerre Legionnaire*", Militaria Magazine, dated September 1986.
Dr. Kurt-Gerhard Klietmann, "*Beiträge zur Geschichte der Auszeichnungen*", Die Ordens Sammlung
Robert Forbes, "*POUR L'EUROPE, The French Volunteers of the Waffen-SS*", 2000.
Rene Chavez, "*LVF – Légion Volontaires Français*", American Philatelist, January 1996.
David Littlejohn, "*Foreign Legions of the Third Reich, Vol 1*", Bender, July 1987.

TITOLI PUBBLICATI - ALREADY PUBLISHING